JOURNALISM IN THE NEW MILLENNIUM

Sing Tao School of Journalism

JOURNALISM IN THE NEW MILLENNIUM

Essays in Celebration of the Sing Tao School of Journalism

EDITED BY DONNA LOGAN

WITH ILLUSTRATIONS BY JOHN Q. LIANG

To Vince,
With deep
appreciation.
Donna Logan

SING TAO SCHOOL OF JOURNALISM
UNIVERSITY OF BRITISH COLUMBIA
VANCOUVER

First published in 1998 by
Sing Tao School of Journalism
University of British Columbia
6388 Crescent Road
Vancouver, British Columbia
V6T 1Z2

10 9 8 7 6 5 4 3 2 1

Canadian Cataloguing in Publication Data

Main entry under title:
Journalism in the new millennium

ISBN 0-88865-545-2

1. Journalism—Canada. 2. Sing Tao School of Journalism. I. Logan, Donna.
II. Liang, John Q. III. Sing Tao School of Journalism.
PN4908.J68 1998 071'.1 C98-910872-4

Edited by Michael Carroll
Designed by Robert R. Reid
Frontispiece photograph by Guy Warrington
Typeset by The Typeworks
Printed and bound in Canada by Comfort Graphics

Contents

vii *Foreword by Martha Piper*

ix *Preface*

1 *Introduction:* **Educating Journalists in Today's World**
Donna Logan

9 **Forging Journalists in the Crucible of the University**
Val Sears

19 **Tensions in Canadian Journalism**
Robert Fulford

29 **Redefining the Role of Daily Newspapers in the Community**
John Cruickshank

39 **Newspapers and the Challenge of the Multimedia Universe**
Peter C. Newman

45 **What It Takes to Be an Investigative Reporter**
Victor Malarek

60 **Politicians, Journalists and the Need for Civil Dialogue**
Shari Graydon and David Mitchell

75 **Courtroom Cameras and the Right to See Justice Done**
Ian Hanomansing

81 **No Good and Evil Please, We're Journalists**
Trina McQueen

91 **The Proliferation of Choice Guarantees Stronger Newspapers**
Conrad M. Black

101 **The Good, the Bad and the Ugly of Corporate Newspaper Control**
Vincent Carlin

113 **Why Newspapers Will Flourish in the Years Ahead**
David Galloway

121 **Keeping Your Head Down on the Firing Line**
Hilary Brown

131 **The Decline of Foreign News in Canada's Media**
Jonathan Manthorpe

144 **How Journalism Struggles to Keep Technology in Its Place**
Jocelyne Côté-O'Hara and Pauline Couture

157 **Pragmatic Objectivity and a New Ethic for Changing Times**
Stephen Ward

167 **Storytelling and the Journalist as Shaman**
Paul Sullivan

177 **News Netiquette in the New Age**
Nicholas Russell

191 **The Write Stuff**
Josh Freed

203 **An Interview with Sally Aw Sian**

Martha Piper B.SC., M.A., PH.D.

Foreword

No one knows my country, neither the stranger nor its own sons... a few lights, a faint glow of our largest city on the vast breast of the night, and all around blackness and emptiness and silence, where no man walks. —Bruce Hutchison, *Canada: The Unknown Country*

BRUCE HUTCHISON—as evidenced by the above excerpt from his first book—was as much a poet as he was an author and journalist. Raised in the Kootenay region of British Columbia and in Victoria, Hutchison ("Hutch") is certainly the greatest journalist to hail from this province, and arguably the greatest this country has produced. His legacy has inspired generations of reporters, columnists and editors in broadcast and print, many of whom have contributed to this book.

The Sing Tao School of Journalism builds on Hutchison's legacy of journalistic excellence and integrity by offering a distinct graduate education from a distinctly western base of operation—the University of British Columbia. By combining graduate study in established academic disciplines with advanced training in the profession, this school becomes one of only three graduate schools of journalism in Canada and the first of its kind west of Ontario.

The school emphasizes scholarly understanding, critical thinking and ethical responsibility. Students will be educated through a rigorous program using the highest standards of research, writing and editing.

The Sing Tao School of Journalism is an important addition to UBC's range of academic programs. Students will draw on knowledge in 12 faculties, 10 schools and more than 100 academic departments, institutes and research centres. This knowledge will find expression in the students' pursuit of excellent journalism.

The new school also grows from external strengths—our links with friends and organizations in Canada and around the world. In particular, we here at UBC extend our great appreciation to the Sing Tao Group for its support and guidance.

Today's information revolution needs qualified journalists. The Sing Tao School of Journalism marks a significant step in the ongoing advancement of accurate, insightful, creative and responsible journalism in Canada. We all look forward to the school's growth and to the professional contributions of its graduates in the years ahead.

MARTHA PIPER
PRESIDENT
UNIVERSITY OF BRITISH COLUMBIA

Preface

THE UNIVERSITY OF BRITISH COLUMBIA, although lacking a school of journalism until the fall of 1998, has a fine tradition of turning out distinguished journalists. A few of the many UBC graduates who went on to make names for themselves as journalists include Allan Fotheringham, *Maclean's* columnist; Pierre Berton, author and journalist; Joe Schlesinger of the CBC; Val Sears of the *Toronto Star* (retired); Hilary Brown of ABC-TV; Vaughn Palmer of the *Vancouver Sun;* and the late Bruce Hutchison, Stuart Keate and Alexander "Sandy" Ross. Their "school of journalism" was the *Ubyssey*, which in 1998 celebrates its 80th year. Throughout that time, it has been regarded as one of the best university newspapers in Canada.

Thanks to the generosity of the Hong Kong–based Sing Tao Group of newspapers, UBC finally has the school of journalism it has wanted for so many years. The graduate school offers a two-year program leading to a master of journalism. It is only the third graduate school of journalism in Canada and the only one west of Ontario. It is housed in a new structure at the corner of Crescent Road and West Mall, which was built with part of the Sing Tao endowment.

The first graduating class will be in the year 2000. It seemed fitting to mark the opening of the school by reflecting on where journalism is headed; thus a number of prominent journalists and publishers were invited to contribute essays on journalism in the new millennium.

Many more journalists and many more subjects could have been included. Unfortunately some of the UBC graduates who were invited to participate were unable to at this time. There will be other occasions. The Sing Tao School of Journalism intends to make publishing one of its primary goals, and it has mounted a Web site for that purpose. A regular monthly publication, the *Thunderbird,* will deal with journalistic issues, and there will be other articles, commentary and analysis in an attempt to establish an ongoing dialogue about the role of the fourth estate.

The school intends to sponsor a number of public lectures and seminars throughout the coming years and will invite prominent journalists and media experts to take part. The first of these was held in September 1998 as part of the official opening of the school. The topic was "Media Wars: The Battle for Your Time." It featured William Thorsell, editor in chief of the *Globe and Mail;* Peter Mansbridge, host of CBC-TV's *The National;* Roger Fidler, author of *Mediamorphosis,* and a professor at Kent State University; and Jeffrey Cole, a leading researcher on the impact of the Internet, and a professor at UCLA.

The authors who have contributed to *Journalism in the New Millennium* are all journalists whom I know and admire. Over the years, I have worked with many of them: Victor Malarek and Josh Freed at the *Montreal Star;* Trina McQueen, Vincent Carlin, Ian Hanomansing, Paul Sullivan and Pauline Couture at the CBC. With the exception of Ian, all of these people are now working for other media organizations.

The group of journalists included in this book represents a wealth of experience. What they have chosen to share, through these essays, will provide invaluable lessons for Sing Tao's students and enjoyable reading for countless others.

There are many people to thank for the realization of this book: the authors, all busy people, who took the time to write thoughtful and thought-provoking essays; Sally Aw Sian, the CEO of the Sing Tao Group, who generously supplied a special grant for this book and the endowment that made the Sing Tao building and the new graduate school of journalism possible; and designer Robert R. Reid, a University of British Columbia graduate, for his excellent book design. One of Robert's previous designs was for *Tuum Est: A History of the University of British Columbia* by the late Dr. Harry T. Logan, my great-uncle, and a longtime classics professor and university historian.

I would also like to thank artist John Q. Liang, for the beautifully done illustrations of the authors in this book; Diane McIntosh, for her creative cover illustration; Michael Carroll, whose outstanding book-editing skills received a challenging workout dealing with the varying styles of more than 20 authors; proofreader Joanne Richardson, who provided the always needed extra pair of eyes; The Typeworks, for their diligent and speedy typesetting; John Rumbolt of Comfort Graphics, who was always cheery, kept incredible deadlines and provided excellent printing services; Sim Lee, my wonderful assistant, who kept track of the budget, paid the bills, faxed, photocopied and generally did anything that was asked of her; and finally Dr. Shirley Neuman, UBC dean of arts, whose support and encouragement was invaluable.

DONNA LOGAN
DIRECTOR AND PROFESSOR
SING TAO SCHOOL OF JOURNALISM

DONNA LOGAN

A graduate of Carleton University in political science and journalism, Donna Logan is professor and founding director of the Sing Tao School of Journalism at the University of British Columbia.

Before her appointment to Sing Tao, she worked at the CBC in a number of capacities: chief journalist and managing editor, national radio news; program director, and then vice president of CBC Radio; vice president, regional broadcasting operations (English/French and Radio/TV); vice president, media accountability; and regional director for British Columbia.

Prior to the CBC, she worked as a journalist and editor for the *Montreal Star.* When it ceased publication in 1979, she was deputy managing editor.

Logan has served on the advisory boards of several Canadian journalism schools and has taught courses and given numerous lectures at Canadian universities and abroad. She is on the boards of the Canadian Journalism Foundation; the Michener Awards for Journalism; the B.C. Newspaper Foundation; and the advisory board of the Canadian Institute for New Media Research and Development.

INTRODUCTION

Educating Journalists in Today's World

All journalists have strong opinions about journalism education. The old-timers who got into the business before journalism schools were ever thought of scoff at the notion, adding that they did fine without a degree in journalism, so why would anyone need one?

Journalism graduates are usually in favour, and there is no doubt that in the past 15 to 20 years, young people have stood a much better chance of getting a job on a newspaper or with a television station if they had a bachelor or master of journalism.

It would be easy to conclude that a journalism degree is the best way to secure a job in the media. The formula, unfortunately, is not quite that simple, and that is why, whenever aspiring journalists have asked for advice, I have agonized over what to tell them.

Over the years, in senior editorial jobs in both print and the electronic media, I tried to analyze what educational background best prepared journalists for their life's work. Was a journalism degree the best route? Was it enough? Should it be taken as an undergraduate or a graduate degree?

These questions still perplex young people interested in working in the media, but they puzzle me less than they used to. Put quite simply: journalists need to know a lot more than journalism. For starters, they have to have something to write about and know how to do it.

As obvious as that sounds, this fact is often overlooked. I remember getting a job as a reporter based on an interview in which the questions were only about journalism. The editor didn't seem concerned whether I knew any history, geography, political science or the myriad other disciplines so critical to informed reporting. Nor did this particular person seem to care if I knew anything about how the major components of society worked. There were no questions about the inner workings of government, politics, the justice system, the business world or the arts, all of which are probably more important than knowing how to write a lead with the requisite who, what, when, where, why and how.

Much later, when I was interviewing people who wanted to become reporters, I broke the questions into three main categories: academic preparation, journalistic knowledge and life experience. All were equally important, but I found myself increasingly drawn to candidates who had actually done something other than journalism before deciding to switch to writing. They brought a perspective that was often missing from graduates fresh out of journalism schools.

While the majority of reporters working in the media today have journalism degrees, the relationship between the industry and journalism schools has been an uneasy one at best. The main complaint seems to be not with the training in journalism per se, but with the lack of knowledge of how a democratic society actually works.

One editor of an influential Canadian daily told me recently that he was considering not hiring any more journalism graduates: "I need people who understand how the justice system works, how public policy is formulated, how the banking system functions, et cetera. In order to do insightful reporting, one has to know the inner workings of society's major institutions, public and private. Otherwise one ends up sniffing around the edges."

The goal is to improve the information base and scholarly knowledge of graduates for reporting and writing in their specialty subject areas.

Comments from industry sources such as the one above, and my own experience, have influenced me greatly in planning the graduate program that will be offered at the Sing Tao School of Journalism. The school is designed for graduate students, preferably people who have already spent some time as working journalists and who want to improve both their journalistic and academic abilities.

One-third of the credits in the two-year program at the Sing Tao School of Journalism will be taken in an academic discipline outside journalism, ideally in the area where the reporter intends to specialize. It can be the arts, science, technology, politics, medicine, law, economics or Asian studies, to name only a few of the choices available.

The goal is to improve the information base and scholarly knowledge of graduates for reporting and writing in their specialty subject areas. In order to achieve this, the school intends to work closely with many other faculties and departments at the University of British Columbia, such as the Faculty of Commerce and Business Administration; the Department of Political Science; the Centre for Applied Ethics; the Faculty of Law; the Centre of Research in Women's Studies and Gender Relations; and the Department of Theatre, Film and Creative Writing.

The academic atmosphere will be distinctly interdisciplinary. Interaction with the outside world will be a high priority and that, too, will be interdisciplinary. The school intends to have not only a steady stream of prominent journalists delivering guest lectures but to expose the students to leaders in government, industry, the public sector and the arts, as well.

One of the many criticisms aimed at journalists is that they are too insular. They hang out together, date one another, sleep together and generally seem to enjoy one another's company. Eventually, it is said, they even start writing for one another.

Journalists often defend themselves against this allegation by saying they have to remain independent, for fear of compromising themselves when it comes to reporting on the activities of someone they have befriended or some organization they have joined. Many journalists belong to no organizations, except for their own professional associations.

Such professional isolation may or may not be necessary, but it can also lead to the journalist getting out of touch with his or her community, a charge that is frequently levelled at today's journalists. At Sing Tao students will be taught the importance of knowing their communities through actual assignments and exposure to people from a wide variety of sectors.

The school plans to examine, through classroom work and research, many of the other issues facing journalists. The industry is experiencing inordinate change, and never has the scrutiny from the public been greater. Everything is being questioned, including the very definition of news.

Driving the change, of course, is technology. Just when newspapers thought they had worked out how to adjust to television, along came the Internet, a whole new medium with vast implications for many sectors of society, none more than newspapers. The school intends to play a leading role in studying the impact of new media on conventional media, i.e., newspapers and television. It will do this through research, seminars, public lectures and forums. And developments such as on-line journalism and journalists, on-line newspapers and magazines and their impact on long-standing news outlets will be examined and debated.

Events involving the public will be an important part of Sing Tao's outreach to the community. Many of the issues being discussed in newsrooms and editorial boardrooms are of deep concern to the public, and although there is an increasing amount of attention given to media matters in the popular press, the public is generally unaware of many of these debates: Is objectivity achievable or any longer desirable? Why is foreign news coverage declining? Why is so much attention paid to pop stars and sports heroes? Do public figures have any rights to privacy? Where is the line between news, analysis and opinion? These are all hot topics in journalistic circles today that could benefit from public input.

To this list could be added topics of particular concern to Canada's West: coverage of the Asia-Pacific region and the central-Canadian bias in media reporting, to mention only two. Because the Sing Tao School of Journalism is only the third graduate journalism school in Canada and the other two—at Carleton University and the University of Western Ontario—are in the East, it makes sense to focus on western media issues.

The school expects to respond to timely developments such as the launch in the fall of 1998 of Conrad Black's new national daily newspaper. What better case study could there be for a group of aspiring journalists? Print journalism, which had been on the decline, is suddenly making a comeback, thanks to the Internet. Not only are conventional newspapers now on-line, but new ones are strictly on-line, with no newsprint edition. Even established papers are reinventing themselves, and circulation is growing.

The Internet has raised many ethical questions pertaining to the practice of journalism.

Newspapers have always been the major generators of news copy, turning out, in a single issue, several times the content of any one television newscast. Now they are seen as providers of information for the Internet. Reporters have always gathered more material than they can possibly use or fit into a newspaper. With the Internet, there is now a place for the overflow. Many newspapers are already offering additional information on their Web sites to stories contained in their newsprint editions.

The Internet has raised many ethical questions pertaining to the practice of journalism. Questions of accuracy and sourcing seem to bother traditional journalists most. They worry that their position will be undermined by upstart "Internet reporters" who think nothing of using rumour and innuendo and who have made a mockery of the standard journalist credo of having two sources for every piece of information.

On the Net, anyone can be a reporter. An unknown like Matt Drudge can suddenly scoop *Newsweek* and the *Washington Post* on the Bill Clinton–Monica Lewinsky story and end up as a guest on *Meet the Press* and be invited to speak at the august Washington Press Club.

With so many issues unfolding and so much change happening, it is difficult to think of a more exciting or challenging time to start a graduate school of journalism. The skills courses at Sing Tao will concentrate on advanced levels of researching, interviewing, reporting, writing and storytelling. Each of these skills is basic to becoming a good journalist, no matter in which medium, but in an increasingly competitive world, storytelling is probably the most essential journalistic tool. If you want the reader's precious time, you need to hook him or her, as Josh Freed points out in his excellent piece on the "write stuff," elsewhere in this book.

But will there be jobs for these graduates? many have asked. The question is understandable, given the downsizing that has taken place in print, radio and television in recent years. Fortunately that trend is largely over and, in fact, the number of jobs with Canadian newspapers actually went up last year. Conrad Black's launch of his national daily has caused other papers to beef up editorial newsrooms in preparation. The proliferation of all-news cable television channels has also led to new jobs. The Internet's "publications" will create new opportunities, and professional journals become more numerous every year.

Whether Sing Tao's graduates are successful in winning any of these jobs in mainstream journalism will depend on whether they can meet the demands of publishers and fit into the voids that exist, for example, in science and technology. If they can't, there is plenty of opportunity on the newly successful community papers, which are also multiplying, or with the alternative press.

It is fortunate that jobs are opening up, because there are no lack of students interested in getting into journalism. The Sing Tao School of Journalism, although brand-new, received 10 times the number of applications it could accept in the first year of its two-year program.

Many did not meet the requirements. The ideal student entering the school will have an undergraduate degree in an appropriate discipline—science, arts, law, fine arts, et cetera—and some journalistic experience. Students without journalistic experience can be admitted, but they must demonstrate an aptitude for the business by writing a manuscript that shows journalistic promise.

Students with undergraduate degrees in journalism will not be excluded, but a baccalaureate in an academic discipline is preferred, in keeping with the belief that journalists need to know more than just journalism.

The program would like to attract some reporters who have been working as generalists for a minimum of five years, with a view to turning them into specialists. Unfortunately the number of journalists who go for further academic study once they secure a job on a newspaper or TV station is few and far between. By the same token, most employers have not been encouraging or even very cooperative with students wishing to take additional studies.

This attitude might be excusable if on-the-job training were abundant, but it is spotty at best in most Canadian and American media organizations. The puzzling element here is that employers who are dissatisfied with their reporters' levels of knowledge don't see fit to invest in upgrading their scholarship. A few fellowships are offered to Canadian journalists for further study, but not nearly enough when you consider the need.

It would be naive to think that journalists can learn all they need to know from a two-year master's program, but it is my hope that the Class of 2000, Sing Tao's first graduating class, will emerge knowing that a commitment to journalism is a pledge to a lifetime of learning.

Essays

VAL SEARS

Val Sears is a graduate in arts of the University of British Columbia (1949) where, in his final year, he was managing editor of the *Ubyssey.* After a year with Canadian Press in Vancouver, he moved to Toronto to take up duties as a reporter-photographer, feature writer and copy editor for the *Telegram* between 1952 and 1959.

In 1960 Sears was hired as an opinion-page editor by the *Toronto Star,* and was subsequently appointed Ottawa bureau chief. Until his retirement from the *Star* in 1991, he served variously as editorial writer and editorial-page editor; European bureau chief; national reporter; Washington, D.C., bureau chief; science editor; political editor; and feature writer.

Sears, who now lives and works as a freelancer in Ottawa, has won two National Newspaper Awards, one for feature writing and another awarded to the *Toronto Star* bureau for political coverage. He has also won a science-writing award, and is the author of a book, *Hello Sweetheart, Get Me Rewrite,* on Canada's newspaper wars in the 1950s.

Forging Journalists in the Crucible of the University

IN THE BEGINNING, there was the *Ubyssey.*

Before interns and scholarships, before radio colleges and television academies, before Canadian Press and Conrad Black, well before the Sing Tao School of Journalism, the *Ubyssey* was the University of British Columbia's remarkable launch site for generations of journalists.

In its 80-year history—the first issue appeared on October 17, 1918—the *Ubyssey* has given hundreds of young men and women a taste for the fascination of news and the basic skills of producing prose under pressure. But in all the student newspaper's long history, it is, arguably, the decade following World War II that produced the most journalists, many of whom became household names.

Consider: Pierre Berton, reporter, author, TV personality and Canada's foremost popular historian; Allan Fotheringham, wit, dandy and national storyteller; John Turner, a *Ubyssey* sports editor who became prime minister; Jack Wasserman, chronicler of Vancouver's streets and high life; Ron Haggart, Toronto columnist and TV producer; Joe Schlesinger; reporter, writer and the CBC's top foreign-affairs analyst; Vaughn Palmer, editor and writer with the *Vancouver Sun;* Danny Stoffman, one of Canada's best magazine journalists; Norm Klenman, television writer and filmmaker and cofounder of television station CKVU in Vancouver; Don Ferguson, Reuters and CBC news executive; George Robertson, longtime CBC-TV producer; Eric Nicol, author and humorist; Senator Pat Carney, among other things, a minister in the government of Prime Minister Brian Mulroney; Alexander "Sandy" Ross, magazine editor and book author. And the list goes on.

Later, when the postwar tide of males began to ebb, the paper graduated a notable series of female writers, among them Hilary Brown, foreign correspondent for ABC-TV, based in London and the eastern Mediterranean; and most recently, Katherine Monk of the *Vancouver Sun.*

But the years from the end of the war to the mid-1950s were an identifiable hothouse time for media talent at the *Ubyssey:* turbulent, productive, casually academic; ink, beer and laughter for the self-proclaimed "Illegitimate Children of the Publications Board." But the reasons for this are a little harder to pin down.

Certainly the postwar atmosphere made a difference. Veterans, older and swaggering, fraternized with acned high-school graduates desperate to prove they were equally tough and sophisticated. The combination, stoked by serious overcrowding and mixed-up courtship rituals, was a volatile one. But in the dungeons of the *Ubyssey,* buried beneath Brock Hall, it was a creative exchange: worldly veterans and youthful talent; the cocky kid on the block and the guy with his arm shot off; mentoring and drive.

There was also, perhaps not uniquely, a dedicated professionalism. This was a newspaper, published four times a week, with all the deadline pressure, editing worries, exhilaration and despair that news, feature and editorial writing imprints for a lifetime.

"We had professional standards," recalls John Turner, then "Chick," sports editor and "Chalk Talk" columnist. "We thought of ourselves as the fourth-largest newspaper in British Columbia after the *Sun, Province* and *News-Herald* [a long-dead Vancouver morning paper]. Many of us had summer jobs with the *Sun.* When I was sports editor, I competed with the *Sun* sports editor for stories."

Student papers can be highjacked by special-interest groups—militant feminists, tree-huggers, ideologues of every sort, even poets.

Pierre Berton says: "There was a kind of joyful ebullience about the place. I learned to write headlines and edit on the *Ubyssey.* I went right to the *News-Herald,* and I was city editor very quickly."

The learning process was never easy, and sometimes the search for accuracy was chastening. A young woman reporter had to be cautioned about fact-checking when, after she turned in a story on the annual Cairn Ceremony, celebrating the pile of stones built on the campus by pioneer students, the editor found she had written: "It was the first student erection on the campus."

Although professionalism may be an obvious goal for journalists-in-training on a student newspaper, it is not always the primary objective. Student papers can be highjacked by special-interest groups—militant feminists, tree-huggers, ideologues of every sort, even poets. Their purpose may be noble, but two pages listing the names of stores to boycott because they carry a dictator's products hardly constitute campus news.

Nor does a communal editorship reflect the real world of brutal newsroom authority. The postwar *Ubyssey* had no such pretensions. Indeed, there was probably more student benefit from the hands-on production of genuine information from typewriter to press than specialization would have allowed. Staff were obliged to shepherd the paper from the campus news desk to Morris Belkin's tiny Kerrisdale print shop, help with the typesetting and emerge ink-stained but triumphant every Tuesday, Wednesday, Thursday and Friday.

"There was a great deal of self-confidence," says Turner. "And pride. And it was fun."

Along with the responsibility of producing a professional, widely read and entertaining newspaper was the freedom to do so. Conservative philosopher and polemicist Russell Kirk, in an essay entitled "The Freedom, Responsibility and Power of the Student Press," makes the point most directly:

> I hold that the student newspaper or magazine ought to enjoy a higher degree of freedom than does the public, commercial publication; that is, the editors and contributors should be secure in a greater latitude of judgement and expression than are the editors and contributors to most periodicals. For the student press should share in the privileges and immunities of academic freedom.
>
> Excesses of zeal, imprudence of judgement, and even intemperance of language ought often to be tolerated in the student press when similar offenses would not be tolerated in the ordinary press: for often it is better that the indiscretions of youthful judgement be endured than that faculty of forming resolute opinions should be discouraged.

Certainly the postwar *Ubyssey* regularly took the position that if a thing was worth doing, it was worth doing to excess. Nor was imprudence of judgement and intemperance of language entirely lacking. This, of course, brought regular clashes both with the funding Alma Mater Society and the administration. But there were few outright defeats for the freedom of the student press.

On one occasion, the *Ubyssey* proposed to publish on its front page a picture of the dean of engineering cavorting with a stripper at an engineering ball. The engineering administration took exception, and the editor of the paper was threatened with expulsion if the picture appeared. In the next edition of the *Ubyssey,* there was a picture-sized blank space with the original cutline describing the joyful exercise and the word *Censored* instead of the picture. A copy of the photo and an explanation was sent to the Vancouver dailies, where it was given nationwide exposure via Canadian Press. This sophomoric broadside was enough to silence even the steel-ringed engineers.

There was, of course, an important negative that contributed to the excellence of the postwar *Ubyssey:* no television.

For all its pervasiveness and power, television does not necessarily require good writing. The 90-second news report or analysis encourages a notebook summary and hair spray rather than a singing sentence. But during the war years, and immediately after, print ruled, alongside radio. Both required words and the ability to find the right ones. Skills such as bringing readable order to the chaos of events, bellowing a coherent story into a telephone in a noisy stadium, and editing and writing headlines to fit available space could only be developed through mentored practice. *Ubyssey* reporters *had* to be good writers if they wanted to make a living in the world of words.

The debate over the role of the student newspaper—professional newspaper versus advocacy journal (the variety of college publications across the country is evidence of its vigour)—is reflected, in measure, by the continuing argument over journalism education: should it take place in trade schools or centres of communications studies? Since journalism schools were established in Canada in the postwar period—Ottawa's Carleton University and London's University of Western Ontario were the first to introduce them—they have quickly taken over from college newspapers as the place to learn and understand the news business. And they have a singular virtue for newspapers, magazines, and radio and television stations: they are handy places to get a professional assessment and to hire print reporters, radio "spit-catchers" and future TV anchors—at least as summer replacements.

But in a job-scarce world,
journalism schools and students have
to grapple with two issues:
what to teach and what to learn.

Journalism itself is also enormously popular. In fact, in some universities it is the most popular of all studies, particularly since Bob Woodward and Carl Bernstein's *Washington Post* Watergate-coverage dramas turned ordinary wordsmiths into heroes. But in a job-scarce world, journalism schools and students have to grapple with two issues: what to teach and what to learn.

In 1947 the United States established a Commission on the Freedom of the Press, whose report still resonates today. The commissioners made it clear that they didn't have much use for the trade-school approach to journalism schools: "We recommend the creation of academic-professional centers of advanced study, research and publication in the field of communications... we doubt that new professional or technical training schools should be established in this [communications] era." But if there were going to be journalism schools, the report writers urged, they ought to be closely associated with "general education ... it is important that students who enter schools of journalism not be deprived of a liberal education." Not surprisingly, a good many universities followed the commission's advice and made a bachelor of arts degree a minimum admission requirement to their journalism schools.

Today, no doubt to give journalism schools academic legitimacy, there appears to be increasing enthusiasm for journalism as a communications study rather than as merely a vocation. Wilbur Schramm was director of the Institute for Communications at Stanford University when he wrote in his book *Responsibility in Mass Communication:*

> Journalism school and other mass communications curricula are not best used when they train students for the first six months of their employment; they should rather prepare their graduates for the years that follow the first six months; not in the skills which enable the young employee to do well at first, but rather the understanding which enables him to do well throughout his career. There is no reason why he should not learn some skills, too; but, whenever there is to be a choice of time between learning the vocational skills and gaining the broad understanding of society and mass communication's place in it, the time should always be used for the broader and less immediately useful studies. The schools should aim for the long, not the short term; for on his job the new man can much more easily learn the skills of his job than he can learn to understand human beings, social organization, economics, and science.

Of course, today's aspiring journalists, while admiring Schramm's logic, might respond, with economist John Maynard Keynes, that "in the long term we are all dead." Or at least still looking for a job.

Nonetheless, there appears to be almost universal agreement among media executives that the men and women they want to hire must have a broad academic background in such subjects as history, English, political science, economics and at least one foreign language. They must also be able to touch-type, a routine skill all too frequently ignored by students planning a curriculum. And a fundamental appreciation of the technical knowledge required for print, radio and TV work is obviously essential.

Vocational skills can be learned rapidly, but academic studies provide something more important: an ability to ask meaningful questions on a variety of subjects, and a degree of confidence in handling the expertise of an interview subject and a network of contacts. The inevitable "How did you feel when...?" may be acceptable in a TV scrum, but it won't do in a more thoughtful environment.

A classic example of what can happen when such abilities are absent is related by American TV reporter Linda Ellerbee. A Chicago newsman, says Ellerbee, asked a bystander how she felt when she saw some scaffolding fall, killing three workmen.

"I didn't feel anything," said the woman. "I didn't see the scaffolding fall."

"Well," asked the reporter, "how would you have felt if you had seen it?"

As if to defend the integrity of TV reporters in general, Ellerbee assures that the offending reporter was fired.

While most journalism schools offer courses in all three media opportunities—print, radio and television—there comes a time when a decision has to be made: print or television. There is a lot more money, power and national influence in television, but there is more personal satisfaction in writing. If an initial choice has to be made, it would seem sensible to opt for print. The basics of television can be learned in a few months; it can take a lifetime to learn to write a proper sentence.

"It is sad," says Cameron Bell, a Vancouver television producer, "that we are getting into a generation of reporters that have never been in print. The people coming out of journalism schools just want to be clerks. They don't embrace the notion of the fourth estate. I want people who will turn ashen-faced if you say, 'Are you sure that's what the quote was?'"

The attitude of media employers toward journalism school graduates is likely changing as more such graduates reach executive, and therefore, hiring positions. But when newspaper editors were surveyed about the value of a journalism education by the Canadian Daily Newspaper Publishers Association in conjunction with the Royal Commission on Newspapers in 1981, their response was "inconclusive." Furthermore, a research study by the commission reported that "Almost half the editors cited the main weakness [of journalism school graduates] as lack of practical skills, including spelling, grammar, typing and interviewing. There was also criticism of journalism graduates as tending to lack background in disciplines other than journalism which would enable them to cope with the increasing trend to specialization within newspapers." And the report cited other weaknesses: "a reluctance to do junior jobs and even general reporting assignments" and "an insistence on plunging headlong into advocacy journalism and to consider objectivity as somehow degrading."

While these criticisms are not directly transferable to news programming on television, there are obvious parallels, particularly the immediate enthusiasm for documentary work and the little joy displayed in doing grunt tasks.

Journalism studies are incredibly time-consuming, especially when the student has to move between TV documentaries, magazine-length articles, radio forums, investigative reports and sex. To the despair of a number of journalism school professors and observers, this frantic rush to pass and start doing bang-bang stuff in Bosnia is at the expense of the most essential ingredient of a journalism education: reading.

If a student doesn't read, he can't write; if he doesn't read, he can't learn; if he doesn't read, he can't steal. This last statement doesn't mean I'm advocating plagiarism, an absolute no-no; it merely refers to the simple filing away of an apt phrase, a telling anecdote, a novel approach, a new word. Journalism is popular communication and requires a constant refuelling of popular idioms before they reach the cliché stage. Books, newspapers, magazines and especially television sitcoms, cop dramas and operating-room sagas are rich sources of contemporary language. The people who write dramas and comedies for television are at the leading edge of popular culture—or they get dumped. There is an educational payoff in drinking beer and watching how they do it. And perhaps doing it better.

If a student doesn't read, he can't write;
if he doesn't read, he can't learn;
if he doesn't read, he can't steal.

Aside from the emphasis on a liberal education as a vital component of a journalist's value, there are a number of handy things the school can teach that the college likely will not: ethics and libel law, for example.

Once past the pyramid lead and the double-ender TV interview, ethics become a significant component of a journalism course. They are easy to teach and inevitably stimulate classroom debate. They can be ignored as simply an academic exercise, but at the serious risk of a failing grade.

Ethics, in the large sense of the responsibility of the press, are important; ethics as a function of the decent thing to do are less so. Most newspeople regard ethical behaviour as a personal matter, and the less involvement with newspaper or station management the better. In any case, classroom debate on ethical positions recedes in the face of an editor's command: Write it or get fired.

There is, however, a great and useful debate on the ethical responsibility of the press. John Fraser, a former editor of *Saturday Night*, wrote on the matter in the *Globe and Mail* a number of years ago:

The notion that somehow cruelty is a journalistic privilege—a right really, almost an obligation—seems to me to be a symptom of the prevailing dysfunction which has afflicted my profession for the past 30 years. And while we're at it, what about "uncontested privilege"? Or the right to be lazy? Or to be vituperative. And then there's the right to fake objectivity and the right to distort facts and quotes—or to ignore them altogether. Such things are part of a journalist's perceived identikit now.

Fraser traces the problem "back to journalism schools, which don't just feed into the post-Watergate cynicism and distrust of anything or anyone worthy of an 'investigative' report or 'in-depth' profile, they positively foster institutional rancour and disbelieving zealotry with a righteousness no longer to be found even in a fundamentalist divinity school." An ethics debate on these terms would no doubt be as useful to journalism professors as it would be to students.

The value of a smattering of libel law in these litigious times is obvious and likely only obtainable—outside of a law school—in an embracing journalism course. It appears that the timeworn libel advice—"when in doubt, leave it out"—is no longer enough.

One feature of daily journalism that schools find most difficult to replicate is deadline pressure. The awful, gut-wrenching feeling of facing a blank screen with 10 minutes to deadline and not a sensible sentence or image in your head is a defining feature of news work. And yet the pressures of a real station or a real newspaper when your job is on the line is nearly impossible to create in an academic atmosphere. One useful approach, however, is that of the University of Regina, where one journalism semester is spent working at a Saskatchewan radio or television station or newspaper at prevailing rates of pay.

Finally it ought to be made clear, once again, that writing, unlike quantum mechanics or brain surgery, is not something that can be entirely learned. You can be shaped as a writer at journalism schools, but you cannot be created. You can either tell a story or you can't. You either love doing it or you don't. If it's no fun, quit.

As Clifton Daniel of the *New York Times* once told a graduating journalism class: "Journalism is a calling—not a trade, not a profession, but a calling."

You've got to hear it.

ROBERT FULFORD

Robert Fulford has been a journalist since he left high school in 1950 to work as a junior sportswriter at the *Globe and Mail.* He now writes a weekly column for the *Globe* on the arts, his main interest for many years. His work appears in such journals as *Toronto Life, Canadian Art, Azure* and *Queen's Quarterly.*

In the 1960s, Fulford wrote a book column five days a week and a Saturday column on art for the *Toronto Star.* He was editor of *Saturday Night* from 1968 to 1987, and has hosted a CBC Radio program and a TVOntario television show.

An Officer of the Order of Canada, Fulford has also received the William Kilbourn Award for lifetime achievement at the Toronto Arts Awards; the Lifetime Achievement Award of the Canadian Journalism Foundation; the Foundation Award for Outstanding Achievement at the National Magazine Awards; and five honorary degrees. His books include *Best Seat in the House* (1988), a book of memoirs; *Accidental City: The Transformation of Toronto* (1995); and *Toronto Discovered* (1998).

Tensions in Canadian Journalism

IN THE WINTER OF 1963, a strike closed down all the newspapers in New York City. I went there to discover what life was like without them, and as a journalist I came back with a humbling conclusion. What New Yorkers missed most were things I had nothing to do with creating. They missed stock-market tables, the schedules of movie houses, TV listings, detailed sports statistics, classified advertising—and crossword puzzles. The worst deprivation was the crossword puzzle. Television couldn't provide it, and New Yorkers found it hard to get through breakfast without their puzzle.

One should always consider the discussion of journalism through a prism of this kind, my own equivalent of the old newspaperman's insistence that we must not take our work too seriously because "tomorrow, they wrap fish in it." On the other hand, we know that we are responsible for creating many of the connections that individuals make with the world, and for helping to shape the whole community's idea of what matters and what doesn't. We should be prepared to analyze and criticize our own profession; we should also be prepared to be surprised by what we learn, and possibly chastened.

Journalists everywhere work under scrutiny, but in Canada the attention focused on our profession takes two specific forms. One is our traditional expectation that journalism will help create and sustain the national community, above all through public broadcasting. The other is the theoretical approach to media, which was developed at the University of Toronto from the 1940s to the 1970s by first Harold Innis and then Marshall McLuhan, an approach that has influenced discussion of mass communications throughout the world.

Innis, whose *Empire and Communications* described how mass media make large societies possible by shrinking distances, a central concern for Canada, was the first scholar to place communications at the centre of history, arguing that we can best understand a civilization by studying the way it explains itself to itself, whether it uses papyrus scrolls or printing. McLuhan magnified and extended Innis's ideas. They both argued that each of the media has its own properties and produces its own unique effects. Only a minority of Canadian journalists know the work of Innis and McLuhan in detail, but over 50 years it has seeped through the profession and influenced all of us. They taught us, if nothing else, a useful level of self-consciousness, and they instructed us to examine the structures of the profession we follow. In this spirit, I have tried to examine Canadian journalism as the product of permanent tensions and conflicting pressures.

In their daily lives, journalists are often called upon to balance opposing forces, a role we frequently find annoying or distracting. This is not to suggest, however, that there is something unnatural or harmful in that process. In journalism, as in most forms of expression, the best work can develop through the resolution of tensions. When we disagree vigorously among ourselves, we are often on the brink of making progress. Philosophy speaks of thesis, antithesis and synthesis; in journalism, our work emerges through a similar process of persistent argument. Within newspapers, magazines and broadcasting networks, and even within production teams assigned to make individual programs, we often disagree about fundamentals—what we should be doing, why we should be doing it, how well we have done it in the past. Those who find this tedious should go off by themselves and try to put out a magazine or a radio program single-handedly. In no time they will be longing for the luxury of an argument.

In journalism, as in most forms of expression, the best work can develop through the resolution of tensions.

In Canadian journalism, three persistent conflicts affect our professional lives. An outsider might imagine the English–French conflict as the most obvious, since the rise of French-Canadian separatism threatens to destroy Canada. But, in fact, that plays only a minor role in the structuring of our journalism, which is conducted in two separate compartments—French-Canadian journalism speaking to French Canadians; English-Canadian journalism relating to English-speaking Canadians. From time to time, the inhabitants of these two distinct worlds may quote each other and comment on each other's opinions, but not in a way that defines their work as a whole. The conflict between English and French obsesses us; it does not shape us.

The three tensions I refer to are between corporate goals and professionalism; between Canada and the United States; and between the demands of the independent ego and the needs of community.

As to the first, most journalists are employees of large corporations, and our work is usually organized and budgeted as part of the corporation's profit-making system. If we look at journalism in this way, it's simply an extension of corporate capitalism—and a valuable extension. Journalism makes advertising possible, and without advertising much of business would dry up. Journalism spreads information among business people, everything from stock-market data to management theories. In good times, such as the late 1990s, media corporations produce handsome profits.

At the same time, however, journalists are professionals, and have developed over the generations certain standards of professional conduct. Like most professionals, they do not always meet their own standards; but those standards, passed on through the culture of the newsroom, are nevertheless part of their consciousness. Journalists see themselves as servants of the truth and servants of the public. Naturally these professional responsibilities will conflict with the goals of their corporate managers; naturally one side will win on certain occasions and the other side on other occasions. And, of course, the biases of those involved in such conflicts will play a part. In general, Canadian journalists tend to identify with the welfare state, with government intervention in the economy, with the sponsors of environment-protection legislation and with labour unions. In short, they are committed to a liberal point of view. Managers and owners often see things differently.

Sometimes it seems that capitalist owners inhibit journalism. But, in this, capitalism is not unique. The fact is, owners of any kind can be an inhibiting force. The Canadian Broadcasting Corporation, our largest news-gathering organization, is owned and maintained by the taxpayers, yet tensions arise between journalists and their managers. In recent years, the greatest tension has resulted from budget cuts. The government, in the name of cost-cutting, has severely curtailed CBC Television and Radio, raising the suspicion that official Ottawa (whether led by Liberals or Conservatives) resents the independence of the CBC journalists and seeks to curb their influence.

In the 1990s, two trends have been reshaping Canadian broadcasting. The first is the decline in significance of the national public networks, the English and the French versions of the CBC, due to funding cuts and broader competition; once the vital centre of Canadian broadcasting, the CBC has for years been moving toward the margin. The second is the rise in the number of channels; in the past 20 years, they have increased from a handful to several dozen, with more to come. It appears we are moving out of the era dominated by big, powerful networks and into a period when the TV audience will be broken into smaller and smaller pieces. The business of television in the late 20th century is beginning to resemble the business of newspapers in the late 19th century.

As for newspapers, they are less numerous and less powerful than they once were in Canada, but they continue to show signs of increasing economic health and in some cases they reach higher levels of professional accomplishment. When Conrad Black obtained control of the Southam chain, journalists viewed the future of Southam's newspapers with trepidation. An old-fashioned press baron, Black is famous for his conservative views, in particular his embrace of market economics, his suspicion of government, his enthusiasm for the United States and his impatience with English-speaking Canada's traditionally relaxed and genial approach to French-Canadian separatism. Many feared that under his control the Southam newspapers would be filled with his views. To an extent, this has happened: papers such as the *Montreal Gazette* now carry right-wing columnists that they would have disdained in the recent past. But Black's importance lies beyond opinion. What matters most about him is that he apparently admires good newspapers, thinks they can make profits and believes in spending money to create them.

Possibly newspapers will begin moving their activities to the Internet, eventually letting their paper editions decline and slowly fade away, at some point a few decades from now.

At the beginning, he promised to improve Southam, which in recent years had grown dull and listless. And in the first years, his performance has been impressive. He has greatly improved the *Ottawa Citizen,* in a way that echoes the *Globe and Mail*'s decision, in the early 1990s, to emphasize interpretation and reflection rather than news. Under Black, the *Montreal Gazette,* the *Vancouver Sun,* and the *Hamilton Spectator* have all demonstrated new energy and ambition. Black's much-discussed plan to create a new national daily in the autumn of 1998 is the best news Canadian print journalists have heard in a generation. Assuming it goes ahead, Toronto will have five daily newspapers, more than any other city in North America, and Canada will have an expanded view of itself and the world. Black may well assume a place in history as one of the most creative of Canadian publishers.

In recent years, technology has posed a new question for the press: Will the Internet replace the daily newspaper printed on paper, the object we hold so easily in the subway or over breakfast? My answer is: Not soon. Most of today's adult readers will remain addicted to news on paper. However, I can imagine a fundamental change. When a generation is reared with computers as part of ordinary life, when screens become much more readable (as they certainly will) and when there's an Internet connection up and running most of the time in most homes—when, that is to say, the Internet becomes as comfortable as the phone or the radio—then electronic newspapers will be able to take over many of the economic functions and some of the editorial functions of the newspaper, perhaps eventually all of them. Possibly newspapers will begin moving their activities to the Internet, eventually letting their paper editions decline and slowly fade away, at some point a few decades from now. Whatever the change, however, the function of journalism will not radically change; nor will its value.

I agree with Keitaro Oguri, the managing editor of the *Asahi Shimbun* Tokyo head office, who addressed this subject in October 1997, during Japan's Newspaper Week. He argued that "the more diversified the means of information transmission, the more their survival hinges on the substance they provide." He cited investigative journalism as work of value that newspapers can offer. I would also say that newspapers should emphasize their historic strengths, which include literary style and the ability to convey information through powerful narrative. (I also agree with Keitaro Oguri's general advice to editors and reporters. He said: "I recommend astute optimism. Stare reality in the eye, deal sternly with injustice, and do not forget to exercise a sense of humour.")

A second focus of tension in Canadian journalism is the relationship with the United States, which we might describe as one-way internationalism. Canadian mass media steadily report on American affairs, political, economic and cultural; in the United States, the mass media do not report on Canadian affairs at all. Canadians may claim this demonstrates that Americans are provincial in their outlook, and that's not entirely wrong. Certainly they tend to ignore foreign countries, unless those countries are troublesome. Moreover, in the era of vastly improved communications, Americans have grown less rather than more interested in foreign countries. Daniel Bell, the eminent social scientist, has made the point that even American intellectuals no longer consider it important to know about the writers of Italy or France; and those who pay careful attention to the film world are painfully aware that the once-vibrant appreciation of international cinema on American university campuses has now largely disappeared. Those who watch the news on U.S. television networks cannot miss the fact that in the 1990s the world it depicts has been steadily contracting. Perhaps this tendency flows from the vastness of America itself. Within its own borders, the United States is a huge and amazingly diverse empire, in which all forms of humanity exist, speaking most of the languages of the world. Americans find this empire so large and complex and engrossing that they have difficulty looking beyond it. I grasped this when I attended an international conference in Hungary in 1985. Publishers of books from countries such as Romania, Denmark and Portugal complained about inequality in their relations with the United States. They consistently translated American books into their languages, but Americans seldom translated books into English from Romanian, Danish, Portuguese, et cetera. The Americans listened, with sympathy but without comprehension. They have so many titles of their own that they feel no need to look for titles elsewhere. Why should they? And the same applies to television: Americans produce so many programs that they don't need even to glance at work from foreign countries. The result is that the whole world watches American television, but America never watches the television of the world; and not one American in a thousand believes this fact is even noteworthy.

In Canada this imbalance takes an exaggerated form. On English-language television, most of the programs come from the United States, and most of the magazines sold in Canada are also American. Canadians own their own newspapers and radio stations, partly because of government regulations; but in general, the cultural marketplace is dominated by Americans. This means that English-speaking Canadians live, culturally, on at least two levels: they follow American events as if they were Americans, and they view Canadian events as, of course, Canadians. Furthermore, a French-Canadian who uses the English language with ease may be thinking on three levels at once: as a Quebecker, as a Canadian and as an American, or at least as a North American, tuned into North America's mass culture.

The U.S.–Canada relationship helps create a serious failure in our journalism: to a remarkable degree, we rely on American sources for foreign news. If there is a crisis in Africa, most of the coverage that reaches Canadians will come through American news services, and to a lesser extent British and French services; only occasionally will Canadians receive foreign news from Canadian reporters on the scene. This fact means that what we know of the world is filtered through the sensibilities and opinions of Washington and New York—and sometimes London or Paris. In this sense, our journalism remains immature, and it's hard to see any prospect for improvement.

Canada has close economic relations with Japan, and cultural relations, as well. But the Canadian media do not employ even one full-time correspondent in Tokyo. If there is a major event in Japan, some Canadian media will send their own reporters, but most will rely on the Americans, the British and the French. If asked why, newspaper editors will cite costs but, in fact, newspaper profits are at record levels. Perhaps the real reason is a lack of curiosity, a provincialism very like the provincialism of which we accuse Americans.

The third source of tension in Canadian journalism arises from the conflict between the individual ego and the requirements of the community. According to some theoretical writings on journalism, our most vital function is the creation and maintenance of the sense of community.

Certainly this theory was demonstrated often in the European settlement of this continent. People would come together, establish the beginnings of government and perhaps start a school; then someone would create a newspaper, and that would help provide the community with identity and distinctiveness. Eventually the newspaper would also draw citizens into larger communities; in Canada that meant the province first and then the nation. This is one way that collections of individuals turn into societies. We can still see it at work in the mass media today: if people accept a television network or a newspaper or a magazine, then they are on the way to accepting the rules of a society.

All of us long for community, and we do our best to find it in our mass media—even, sometimes, in tabloid journalism.

Alexis de Tocqueville wrote in 1833 that in a secular society government must persuade everyone that they serve their private interests by voluntarily joining their efforts with the efforts of all others. And, "That cannot be done habitually and conveniently without the help of a newspaper." But he also said: "A newspaper can survive only if it gives publicity to feelings or principles common" to large numbers of citizens. And finally: "A newspaper always represents an association whose members are its regular readers." Much the same applies, 165 years later, to everything from radio stations to chat rooms on the Internet. All of us long for community, and we do our best to find it in our mass media—even, sometimes, in tabloid journalism.

In Canada the *Sun* newspapers provide a vivid illustration. The first of them, the *Toronto Sun*, appeared in 1971, following the death of an older broadsheet newspaper, the *Telegram*. A few of the newly displaced employees started their own tabloid, without really knowing how to do it; not one of them had ever worked on a tabloid in the United States or Britain. Slowly they evolved a new way of finding a public.

From the start, they broke the most important rule many of us learned as young reporters: never write about yourself. The people at the *Toronto Sun* wrote constantly about themselves, dramatizing their struggle to become established, casting themselves in the seriocomic role of heroic independent entrepreneur/journalists, turning their efforts (more or less spontaneously) into a newsprint version of a TV sitcom. They wrote about their love affairs, their hangovers and even their competitive feelings toward one another—subjects considered taboo everywhere else in Canadian journalism. When the *Sun*'s editor, Peter Worthington, had two heart attacks and a bypass operation, he wrote a six-part series on his experience. When he sought a parliamentary nomination, half a dozen of his columnists—in flagrant breach of any conceivable conflict-of-interest rules—gave their views on his qualifications and his campaign.

The *Toronto Sun* was personal and emotional, and soon successful. Its editors and writers caught something in the air, perhaps a need for more direct address to the reader, perhaps a desire for a more sentimental journalism; possibly they satisfied a need similar to the feeling expressed in 1997 by the wave of emotionalism over the death of the Princess of Wales. On this basis, the *Sun* became the first new daily newspaper firmly established in North America in more than three decades, a phenomenal performance. Today it flourishes still, with satellite newspapers in three other cities. At the beginning, I disliked it, and I dislike most of it to this minute. But the editors who created it knew something I didn't know about the desires of the public. What they produced was a kind of antidote to urban alienation, a special kind of human association—and an illustration of the way media create communities.

Why, then, is there tension between the individual journalist and the community? It seems to me that this tension arises inevitably in human relations as we balance our own need for self-expression with what the community requires from us. We see it played out most obviously in journalism because journalism is by its nature public. We all develop as individuals, but we find satisfaction in our relations with others. The self grows in freedom and independence, but must be fulfilled through community—in "the interplay," as the great American critic Lionel Trilling put it, "between an awareness of the self that must be saved and developed, and an awareness that the self is yet fulfilled only in community."

Our profession, which feeds on the tumultuous nature of public affairs, is itself in more or less constant tumult. We are at the mercy of swiftly developing electronic technology, abrupt changes in ownership and the vagaries of public taste. Those who have persisted in journalism know that there's rarely a time when we are not under some form of dire threat. We also know that we are rarely without some form of opportunity. Jane Jacobs, a journalist who became a great theorist of city life with her book, *The Death and Life of Great American Cities,* says, "Let's remember that it's always the best of times and the worst of times."

In the midst of this tumult, if we manage to deliver to the citizens a reasonably complete and reasonably independent account of reality, it must be because our profession attracts enough individuals who believe it is worth their while to find out the truth and make it both public and coherent, whatever the obstacles.

JOHN CRUICKSHANK

John Cruickshank is a career newspaperman who has reported and edited with newspapers in Kingston, Montreal and Toronto. He worked as a national correspondent for the *Globe and Mail* in the 1980s and later served on its editorial board and as a foreign-affairs columnist. After three years as managing editor of the *Globe and Mail,* he joined the *Vancouver Sun* in September 1995 as editor in chief.

Cruickshank is married to magazine writer Jennifer Hunter. They have two children.

Redefining the Role of Daily Newspapers in the Community

HERE IS A contemporary paradox that lovers of learning, journalism and democracy should ponder: Canada's newspapers today employ the best educated, best paid, most secure and most diverse generation of reporters, editors, artists, photographers and executives in history. And yet, in this generation, Canadian daily newspapers have been slowly but steadily losing the affection and attention of their communities.

Twenty-five years ago, 80 percent of Canadian households received a daily newspaper. By the late 1990s, that number had fallen to just over half the nation's homes. While Canada's population has continued to rise, daily newspaper circulation has slid from its 1989 peak and is now at a level lower than it was 15 years ago. On any given day in Vancouver, according to a recent survey, one out of two employed women will not even glance at a daily newspaper. Only middle-aged, affluent, educated men can now be counted on to read newspapers regularly.

The reasons the newspaper industry conventionally cites for its declining reach are that people are too busy now to read—too time-poor—and that today's young people are computer junkies, not readers. While there is a grain of truth in both assertions, these are excuses, not unquestionable truths.

In fact, Canadians are not reading less; their reading habits have simply changed. They are far more likely today to be reading a community paper than 20 years ago—or browsing the text-heavy pages of the Internet. They are just not going to daily papers with the frequency or enthusiasm they once did.

A more genuine reason for the long, slow skid of the metropolitan dailies is that they have lost their dominance in key areas of news and advertising. Studies conducted over the past decade and a half by Michael Adams and Donna Dasko at Environics Research in Toronto have found that a steadily increasing number and percentage of Canadians believe that television provides more credible national and international news reporting than newspapers.

By the 1990s, a majority of viewers and readers told Environics that television is the authoritative source for big-picture news. Newspaper journalists greet these findings with incredulity or despair. Clearly television wins the sports category. It shows the games and now offers golf and auto-racing channels. Since the launch of *Entertainment Tonight* and its many clones, television has also undeniably dominated the entertainment-news category. The new niching through cable is also providing magazinelike specialization in lifestyles and business coverage.

It is harder to accept that television news, which manifestly presents fewer and sketchier national and international stories, often going little deeper than a headline, should win the approval of viewers and readers for its work in those areas. But as significant as that injury to their status and authority is, Canadian dailies have suffered far more serious losses to community papers in the competition to provide readers with the kind of local news and advertising they need and want.

Until the late 1970s, community newspapers were still largely a small-town phenomenon. That has changed dramatically. The weekly circulation of Canadian ethnic, community and consumer papers grew by almost 250 percent between 1980 and 1997. In British Columbia that progress has been even more rapid. New technology lowered the entry costs to publishing, but the community and consumer publications won reader and advertiser acceptance by offering neighbourhood news and local ads that the dailies couldn't or wouldn't match.

Community papers typically provide a fraction of the serious editorial content of the dailies.

To a considerable extent, the Canadian metropolitan dailies simply failed to address the competition. They continued to concentrate their news resources on mainstream, downtown issues, and their advertising forces on the largest, most lucrative accounts, virtually ceding the suburbs, where all the growth was happening, to their much smaller and less-sophisticated rivals.

By daily newspaper standards, the community papers did everything wrong. They featured big photos of ribbon cuttings and cheque presentations. They investigated traffic problems, school overcrowding and local pollution. They covered high-school sports and graduation ceremonies. And they did it all on sweatshop budgets and in nonunion newsrooms, while breaking every rule in the business about printing news releases, taking junkets and establishing an appropriate distance between editorial and advertiser.

To finance editorial, they jammed their pages full of ads the size of business cards from restaurants, barber shops and handymen who couldn't afford the dailies' lineage rates. And while the dailies' circulation slumped, community and consumer papers saw their sales figures skyrocket. While the dailies' share of the total Canadian advertising market dropped throughout the 1980s and 1990s, the community weeklies held their slice of total national spending.

According to the standards daily journalists employ to evaluate quality work and what readers need and want, this trend shouldn't be happening. Community papers typically provide a fraction of the serious editorial content of the dailies. Television lurches from photogenic disaster to disaster, rarely providing context, background or any of the journalism of record so favoured by print reporters and editors. The Internet, which has captured the imagination of many young people and some expert readers looking for very specialized news, is vast and rich but frustratingly unedited.

The success of television, the tabloids, community papers and the Internet has led many daily newspaper journalists to become cynical about their readers. Some editors have responded by moving their papers downmarket, taking on the tabloids in the journalism of sensation. Others have tried the superstore model of newspapering, offering something to every demographic group, subgroup and sub-subgroup that their marketing departments can identify.

Disappointed by what they understand of public taste and contemptuous of their editors, many reporters now feel detached from the fate of their papers. Having lost their sense of connectedness to readers and their spirit of common purpose with their colleagues, they work primarily for themselves, deriving their job satisfaction from their professionalism.

Daily newspapers have many excellences. They are both broad in their coverage areas and deep in their analysis compared to their rivals. Their newsrooms are far larger than those of television or the community newspapers, and new high-speed colour presses allow them to produce attractive, exciting-looking pages.

So why are so few dailies growing with their communities? Some journalists believe that the diversity of the Canadian population today is so great that a real mass market no longer exists. They believe that the reading market is so fragmented that it can only be successfully served by many narrowly specialized daily and weekly publications. But this is a declaration of defeat, not the product of analysis. While Canada's social cohesion may be less pronounced now than during earlier periods, the historical strength of newspapers has been in binding diverse groups together.

The modern newspaper—once it became more than a partisan political tract—has only ever succeeded when it created a coalition of disparate readers. One of the newspaper's most significant contributions to civic life has been to provide different ethnic groups, social classes and city neighbourhoods with a common account of the latest news and opinion. When it succeeds, the metropolitan daily draws the broadest possible representation from the many communities within its readership into a daily conversation about the culture.

This ability has the civic benefit of uniting disparate communities in an ongoing dialogue that is protected in our democracies. Freedom of the press is the freedom that every citizen has to be informed and to participate in the daily conversation.

Some people understand this concept in a very simple-minded way and want to treat daily newspapers as a public utility. They are constantly seeking to regulate the press, as if it were a close cousin to the telecommunications business or the waste-disposal industry. They are too often abetted by some journalists who cultivate their public role with a ponderous self-seriousness. These are the reporters and editors who see themselves as civil servants—assistant deputy ministers with press passes. They are priests in the cult of the "newspaper of record."

A day full of news ladled out by the Canadian media is, by and large, a day full of sameness.

Once a clutch of reporters has asserted that newspapers have a "moral obligation" to cover the deliberations of the all-party parliamentary committee on the future of flood-plain management, it is a small step to making it a mandatory responsibility enforceable by the provincial press council. Nothing will kill the public conversation faster. This attitude is a symptom of the detachment that many journalists have from the true needs and interests of the potential readers in their communities. It misses the fact that daily newspapers must sustain the engagement of their community in order to succeed. They must have the wit, intelligence, broad public and social interest, and sense of humour to keep our conversation about the culture going. It is not enough for them to be engaged in public life; they must *be* engaging.

More striking than the growing diversity of the readership is the growing uniformity of newspapers and newspaper organizations. This development may be the result of the modern drive within newspapers for professionalism and sophistication. Virtually all new recruits to metropolitan papers in Canada have completed at least one university degree. Many boast graduate training in journalism in addition to academic work. Journalists' organizations committed to training and the promulgation of professional standards exist at both national and provincial levels. Reporters and editors are widely read and travelled and look to national newspapers, such as the *New York Times* and the *Globe and Mail*, for their models of news coverage—even, frequently, for their daily news agenda.

Large Canadian newsrooms are almost all unionized, and reporters and editors are well paid and enjoy high levels of job protection. Newspapering is seen by its practitioners as a profession, and it is now firmly lodged among white-collar jobs such as social work and teaching. Newspaper management has also become more professional. Publishers who owned newspapers to promote personal visions have been succeeded by manager-publishers who answer for their papers' results to owners and their boards of directors.

In the 1980s and 1990s, it became routine to talk of newspapers as manufactured goods and readers as customers. The same techniques of marketing and distribution that were applied to packaged goods were adapted to newspapers. This standardization of practices nationally—and continentally—may be one of the reasons that daily newspapers in recent years have had such a placeless, generic feel. A day full of news ladled out by the Canadian media is, by and large, a day full of sameness.

The range of stories from coast to coast is oddly narrow. The ambit of formats and techniques in approaching and presenting the news is more straitened still. Most Canadian broadsheet papers have such a similar look that they might have been designed by the same committee of artists. Even the emotional and intellectual range of the daily news is tightly constricted. There is a smattering of sarcasm and irony but almost no belly-laugh humour. There is some analysis of the big stories of the day but almost nothing ever appears in a daily paper that requires hard thinking.

Outside of its day-to-day, often superficial, coverage of the arguments of politicians, the Canadian media almost entirely ignore the ideas and convictions that animate the intellectual lives of the most creative Canadians in cultural, business, religious and academic life. (Despite the apparent overlap of interests between universities and newspapers as social institutions, the cooperation between them in Canada is painfully shallow. The growth of university programs in journalism, and the development of a cadre of professors with experience in both worlds, so far has done little to deepen the connection.)

Occasionally newspapers will provide a glimpse of real tragedy in plain reports of human experience. But, more often, journalists choose to serve as conduits for the never-diminishing flood of stories that document in numbing detail the carnage wrought in plane crashes, train wrecks, ferry sinkings and violent crime. Sex, when it sneaks into newspapers at all, appears in the "Life" or "Family" sections, where it can be discussed in cool, hushed tones by therapists.

With a few exhilarating exceptions, this constricted news agenda and uniform approach varies little from city to city or province to province, as though the home communities of our newspapers had no distinction. News is treated as something generic and abstract. If our newspapers were as different as our communities, or our news agenda as broad and diverse as the lived experience of Canadians, they would be very distinct.

This narrowness is not the product of objectivity or lack of bias. An objective portrayal of our communities would at least show us their differences. The problem is that newspapers are all biased, more or less, in much the same way.

The Canadian media, particularly newspapers, are obsessed with institutions, especially government ones. By sheer weight of coverage, our media say that government is the most significant issue in the lives of Canadians. Government is covered for initiating programs or faulted for failing to introduce them.

Editors typically reply that newspapers just report the news, good or bad, so don't blame them.

The lives of our institutions are the main subjects of the front sections of daily newspapers. We print endless stories about funding, cutbacks, obscure squabbles between government experts and interest groups, speculations about who is to blame when things go wrong. These sometimes have the look of public-policy pieces, but true public-policy pieces are about people, not government funding or regulations. People and places are somehow less relevant, less real, on our pages. Sometimes they are even beside the point.

Daily newspapers often appear out of touch with their readers. This deficiency is not a matter of sloth or ignorance; it is far too uniform an experience across Canada, indeed throughout North America, to be a simple failing. Instead, it seems that some aspect of the professional training or the values of daily journalism today is leading journalists away from readers rather than toward them.

Nothing illuminates the problem at newspapers quite so starkly as the feebleness of journalism's response to the most frequent and recurrent complaint made about the daily news—that it is too negative. Editors typically reply that newspapers just report the news, good or bad, so don't blame them.

Readers think this is nonsense. They believe the news agenda that dominates most daily newspapers is more like a set of ruts on the road of reality than a thoughtful reflection of what is really going on in the world. Many women, young people and minority groups believe the news choices at more than a few daily newspapers are distinctly outdated. They believe these choices reflect outdated assumptions and reflexes of journalists who are insulated from many aspects of social change by their affluence, habits, perhaps even gender.

The inability of daily newspapers to offer a rationale for their news choices leads readers to suspect that the press is exploiting the unhappiness of their communities "just to sell papers." They often view the fourth estate as a parasitic feeder on their problems, not as a partner in exposing the truth and canvassing options for social betterment. They intuit that their newspapers are about, but not for, their communities. They know that journalists report stories because they have heard them, not because they believe they are true. They see the doctrine of objectivity as cloaking a fundamental indifference to the pain and confusion that reporting can cause.

The great strength of community newspapers is that they speak with the voices of their communities. But this is also their greatest weakness. They lack the authority to provide the leadership on critical issues and, as a result, don't have the commitment to intense reporting and editing. In other words, they are too much *of* the community to be a genuine forum for vigorous debate and dispute.

Nobody wants daily newspapers that indulge in boosterism. Nobody wants daily newspapers that turn their backs on the dark corners of their communities. But readers want to feel that their newspapers are committed to them. They know their newspapers can be influential, and they resent the fact that their papers sit on the sidelines most of the time. They are puzzled by columnists who preach rather than report and reason, by reporters who don't investigate the most intense urban problems, by editorial boards that don't take a strong position on the major issues of the day.

Some daily newspapers have started to take on these deficiencies through what has been termed "public journalism." They run editorial campaigns to encourage a larger number of citizens to vote, and conduct organized civic forums to debate development problems.

As a starting point, metropolitan newspapers need to declare their independence from the rest of the world and regain their sense of the distinctiveness of their people and their place. Great metropolitan journalism begins and ends with the unique circumstances of people and places, not with issues and institutions.

Metropolitan dailies have to be entertaining, surprising, passionate and thought-provoking in ways that flow from the lived experiences in their communities. They must recognize that they can be powerful and that they must use their power. (Most papers are a little rusty. It's been a while since the days of the great campaigning papers.)

Above all, they need to find ways of opening their pages to the voices of their readers. They have to be the centre for debate in their communities, the place where the daily conversation about the culture happens. How will we know when this is happening? When North American dailies start to develop distinctive appearances, sections, columns and beats.

Great newspapers already have this distinction. We recognize instantly the style of the *New York Times,* the *Los Angeles Times,* the *Washington Post,* the *Wall Street Journal,* Britain's *Telegraph* and *Times,* and the *Globe and Mail* here in Canada. But aping publications that have a style and distinctiveness is a sure route to failure. Each metropolitan daily has to invent itself through a renewal in its relationship with its own readers and its own community.

Does it matter? Do daily newspapers play such a unique role in our communities that we should concern ourselves about their apparent weakening? Although I am certainly biased when it comes to this question, I still think there is only one possible answer: Yes, it does matter.

Newspapers share with radio and television an ability to build broad audiences—coalitions of readers that cut across all demographic categories. Like the Internet and the other evolving electronic media, newspapers have a capacity to be interactive through their letters to the editor and guest columns and their ability to consult their readers through fax-back and telephone polls. What distinguishes them in a way that should matter to citizens concerned with learning and democracy is that they are capable of communicating serious ideas and arguments. As Louis Rossetto, founder of *Wired,* put it: "The cool thing about print is that it is sensual. The other part of it is that it can convey thought. High thought content is rarely found in any other media than paper."

Daily newspapers are critical because they can be a forum for a thoughtful, ongoing conversation about the culture that engages a large portion of the citizens of each community. They can both document and lead. They can play both a critical and creative role. They can be both for and about their communities.

That's where the real stories are, not in the dry, incestuous debates of the legislature in Victoria or the House of Commons in Ottawa.

Any successful newspaper must echo and articulate the half-formed, but deeply felt, intuitions of its readers, voicing underlying themes about which they themselves may only be dimly aware. The most important of these is the beleaguered condition most ordinary citizens feel in the face of the tidal wave of new and strange technology that creates a sense of being buffeted or backed into a corner by external forces over which they have no control.

First, the character of newspapers—not just the Sun, but all of them—ought to shift more to interpretive reporting, instead of news.

With the age of consensus ending, it will be increasingly difficult for newspapers to retain the confidence of reader-audiences of infinitely diverse views that are being split into ever smaller segments. The more society divides into such irreconcilable fragments, the harder it will be to retain the universal credibility that produces great and relevant city dailies. Ultimately every reader will want his or her own edition, which is what he or she can already get over the Internet—and that medium is still in its infancy.

A general-interest publication like the *Sun* can only thrive if its readers believe the paper is fair, accurate, useful and authentic. (I am deliberately staying away from the concept of objectivity because I believe it is meaningless. Only the dead are totally objective; the rest of us have thoughts and emotions that by definition add a multitude of subjective elements to any piece of journalism, however blandly intended.)

If the *Sun* is to remain the house organ of a society whose fragments are increasingly intolerant of one another, it must keep tuned to its readers' impulses and inclinations. In the past, it has attempted to do this by being overwhelmingly middle-class and trying to please everybody. That doesn't work anymore.

It will take a concerted effort to achieve what was once done by osmosis. A makeover such as the initiative in 1997 was an ideal moment for the *Sun* to reach out for a new mandate. That momentum is still there, ready to be harnessed, but it has not been followed through.

How can the *Sun*—or any other newspaper—remain the voice of urban populism while at the same time moving out in front of its readers to provide greater relevance to their lives?

Having stated my slightly heretical theory, I have some specific suggestions. First, the character of newspapers—not just the *Sun,* but all of them—ought to shift more to interpretive reporting, instead of news. Intelligently assigned and generously budgeted investigative teams would allow the paper to create news instead of simply summarizing or synthesizing it.

If we have lost our mandate as the first carriers of news, let's become carriers of hope, providing practical hints on how to get through the day—and the night.

Second, newspapers must begin to sort out the significant from the trivial. We can't continue to throw everything at readers and hope they will take the time to wade through it. They won't. In selling them a newspaper, we aren't competing for the loonie or more it costs for readers to buy it, but we damn well are competing for the time we can get them to spend reading it.

Third, we must *make* more news. Interpretive reporting should be based not on reporters' editorializing but on digging out ever more relevant facts, and when warranted, publishing substantiated accusations. Any journalist's most essential talent is the creation of interest. That, not sensationalism for its own sake, must become any great newspaper's driving purpose.

Four, we must begin to realize that there are no average readers; there are only common interests—issues and events in which all of us have a common stake. The *Vancouver Sun* must become a newspaper that allows the community to speak to itself—a voice that echoes from grass roots to community leaders and back again—in those primary directions. (People and local institutions communicating with one another through the pages of the *Sun*—just like the Internet!)

Five, we must seriously shift the emphasis from covering "news" (instant stories that are one-day wonders) to explaining "situations" (medium-term underlying community issues that develop over time), describing the options and processes at work. That will require an essential decision. Should the *Sun* continue to go for multiple audiences—many newspapers in one—or develop priorities and a dominant image? Any change—and there must be one—would require conceding certain things to television and radio. If readers devoted more time to the *Sun*, we could make them a clear promise: so doing would reduce the present barrage of noise assaulting their senses. They would become part of the calmer, more specialized world that newspapers cover best.

Six, newspapers must explore more deeply the notion of becoming daily ombudsmen for their readers. They should give advice, succour and useful hints to help people stay afloat, with platoons of specialists—a doctor, a lawyer, a social worker, a consumer expert, a financial adviser, a spiritual guru and others—directly handling readers' queries and concerns. That would make newspapers useful again. If we have lost our mandate as the first carriers of news, let's become carriers of hope, providing practical hints on how to get through the day—and the night.

Seven, the old distinction between writers and readers ought to be redefined. Readers should write more for other readers—i.e., ratepayers' groups, environmental activists, the "poor," the lobbyists, nursery school teachers and mothers, the police, the unions and even striking doctors. They should all have their say. Unprofessional journalism it may be, but new voices, new ideas and more emotional involvement with the paper will be the result. And that, surely, is what's required.

Eight, editors ought to make it easier for readers to obtain back stories or files on certain issues, such as e-mail kits that help make the U.S.-Canada salmon treaty or Bill Vander Zalm's rhetoric more understandable.

Nine, the implicit and barely discernible process operating between editors and readers of newspapers needs closer examination. What image of the reader exists in the mind of the editor when he or she is making up the front page, for example?

Does the *Sun*, in fact, get the quality of audience it deserves? I doubt it.

Perhaps editors ought to imagine that they are the readers' executive assistants, bringing the right things to their bosses' attention in an organized, discreet manner. The front page cannot and should not be a place where there is "something for everybody."

The current philosophy of publishing, not merely at the *Sun* but at all newspapers, is too often limited to derivative premises adapted from the premedia period. In the British tradition, politics was perceived as the manoeuvre of counterweights to inhibit or prevent tyrannical rule. A free society was one in which tyrants were nipped in the bud or headed off at the pass by a free press.

Modern media have developed very little beyond such primitive and barely relevant notions in articulating a coherent philosophy of publishing. Their basic function in modern society ought to be redefined. Now. Before it's too late.

Media, in my view, are the essential arteries of community, literally mediating and transmitting the elements that tie together its social structure. Ideally the *Sun* ought to become Vancouver's central nervous system—politically, culturally and every which way but up.

The *Vancouver Sun* must reestablish itself as the most important source of information in Vancouver—and every city daily in the country must do the same. This can only be accomplished by acknowledging the fact that the "newspaper," as such, has become an oxymoron.

I rest my case.

VICTOR MALAREK

A journalist for three decades and currently a co-host of the CBC-TV's award-winning current-affairs show *the fifth estate,* Victor Malarek has often been described as a crusading reporter. He began his career in journalism as a copy boy at *Weekend* magazine in Montreal in 1968. Two years later, he joined the *Montreal Star* as a police reporter and was one of the first journalists to report on the 1970 FLQ October Crisis.

In 1976 Malarek joined the *Globe and Mail,* where he garnered three prestigious Michener Awards for Journalism. He has written four acclaimed books: *Hey, Malarek!, Haven's Gate, Merchants of Misery* and *Gut Instinct: The Making of an Investigative Reporter.*

Hey, Malarek! documents his troubled and tumultuous childhood and teenage years while in the so-called care of the Quebec child-welfare system. It was made into a feature film in 1988, and in 1991-92 aired on CBC-TV as a drama series entitled *Urban Angel.*

In February 1997, Malarek was awarded the Gemini Award as Best Overall Broadcast Journalist in Canada.

What It Takes to Be an Investigative Reporter

INVESTIGATIVE JOURNALISM is without question the news media's most precious asset. It is society's watchdog, playing a vital role in a free and democratic society. And while journalistic sleuths cannot be expected to expose every scandal, their very presence keeps government officials, corporate CEOs, powerful individuals and unsavoury characters glancing warily over their shoulders.

But the chatter in the nation's newsrooms is that this kind of journalism is hobbling along on crutches and that investigative reporters are a dying breed. Fewer and fewer journalists are being given the time and the tools to dig for meaningful, newsworthy stories. Instead, they are being sent on assignments that are often trivial, flashy and stupid. And then they go a step further by trying to make them sound important.

There are a host of excuses for the lamentable condition that investigative journalism finds itself in today. The most common is the expense and time involved in doing investigations. But that argument falls flat when I look back at the vast majority of investigations I've taken on over the years. They were done on the cheap through hard legwork, and by cultivating solid contacts and trustworthy sources during my years in the business. Often all these investigations took were a few phone calls to steer me onto the right trail. And they were also inexpensive because I knew where to hunt for information and how to use Access to Information and Freedom of Information laws. Again, this comes from experience.

However, to do the really difficult, complex stories, it does take time and money. There is no way around it. Investigative stories like the Airbus scandal unearthed by the CBC current-affairs show *the fifth estate* could not have been done on a shoestring budget. In probes like this, involving the payment of secret commissions in the sale of Airbus airplanes to Air Canada, there are extremely jittery sources to cultivate and very complicated paper trails that circumnavigate the globe. All this takes a serious investment in time, travel and money. One hasty step, one cut corner, could jeopardize the entire investigation and result in a costly lawsuit.

Sadly, when confronted with a probe that offers a degree of difficulty, most newspaper editors and TV news producers fold. Instead, they settle on the safe, secure route and stick with the regurgitated and the mundane. This intransigent attitude really has more to do with laziness and lack of motivation on the part of editors, producers and reporters. It takes tremendous effort to get an investigation under way. It means developing solid sources and contacts, and convincing them to trust you with any information they supply. Then there are seemingly endless pitfalls: slammed doors, threats of libel, and dead ends. It's enough to chill a seasoned veteran. So without the backing of the bosses, it's often not worth the fight.

What troubles me deeply about the hapless direction of investigative journalism is who is picking up the microscope. More and more, we see government-appointed investigators becoming the real sleuths. Imagine men in Tip Top Tailor suits blowing the whistle on government waste, inane management practices and political interference! Yet increasingly it is these investigators who are squirrelled away in back offices sifting through endless sheaves of documents and doggedly following a meandering and oftentimes frustrating paper trail—a trail wide open to journalists.

There is nothing more disingenuous than seeing stories dressed up as investigative reporting that are based solely on leaked government reports.

Instead, it seems that the news media is content to grab on to the reins of these government investigators, taking interest only when the official report is about to be released publicly. Then all the stops are pulled out and packs of journalists are unleashed with one objective in mind—get the report leaked to them in advance so they can boast they got it first. What a journalistic coup! There is nothing more disingenuous than seeing stories dressed up as investigative reporting that are based solely on leaked government reports. And while the fourth estate gladly carries the ink buckets for these investigators, it almost never works in reverse.

Still, as thorough as these government investigators might be, this is certainly no cause for journalists to sit back and lackadaisically wait for the next release. There are plenty of important stories that these straitlaced gumshoes overlook or would never even tackle. And I'm proud to say that, over the years, those kind of stories have been broken by investigative journalists. Among them: the scandal involving the Canadian Airborne Division during its United

Nations peacekeeping mission to Somalia; the sordid and clandestine role of the Canadian Security Intelligence Service in the setting up of the racist Heritage Front; the ineptitude of the police investigation in the wrongful conviction of Guy Paul Morin in the murder of nine-year-old Christine Jessop; and the exposure of the U.S.-government fabricated story of Iraqi soldiers butchering babies who were in incubators at a hospital in Kuwait.

These stories showcase investigative journalism at its best, and they were uncovered through the dogged efforts of reporters who see their work as more than just a job. To them, it's a calling. But stories of this calibre are few and far between. In fact, over the past decade, it has been a rare moment in the House of Commons to hear a member of the Opposition raise a question citing an investigation by a journalist. That's a sad comment on the state of investigative journalism.

One reason for this sorry state is the way editors assign their reporters. Go to a news event anywhere in the country and you'll find scores of journalists tripping over themselves, all chasing the same quote and producing virtually identical stories. It's called pack journalism, and what they do is basic stenography.

Nowhere is this kind of journalism more apparent than on Parliament Hill in Ottawa and in the provincial legislatures and city halls across the country. Every day herds of newshounds scamper from one event to the next, covering the same story, asking the most basic questions and nodding their heads in unison as if they actually understand what is going on. There is no probing, no challenging, just a regurgitation of what they are told. There is an inherent danger in this kind of reporting, and I got my first bitter taste in the fall of 1985 while on assignment in Ottawa for the *Globe and Mail.*

I was assigned to cover what journalists ruefully refer to as a dog-and-pony show. These are events staged by political parties, lobby groups and government departments to get maximum coverage in the news media with minimal risk of negative fallout. I landed a spectacle put on by the immigration department.

Once a year, a cluster of puffy bureaucrats from the department hike over to a spacious conference room in the House of Commons. There they meet with their political masters, members of the Parliamentary Standing Committee on Labour, Employment and Immigration, to explain their good works over the past 365 days. With them they lug reams of documents, flow charts and graphs illustrating just how well the department is running.

On this particular day, the civil servants were trumpeting their crown jewel—the entrepreneur program for wealthy immigrants. From the flashy presentation, it appeared that since its auspicious launch in 1978, the program was a smashing success. Every year since, thousands of well-heeled foreigners and their families had been ushered to the front of the line and welcomed to Canada on the promise that they would each invest hundreds of thousands of dollars in businesses and create tens of thousands of jobs for unemployed Canadians.

Given the glossy charts, soaring graphs and starry statistics, the program could hardly be knocked. Scores of businesses, large and small, had been established right across the land, putting hard-pressed Canadians to work. The presentation was a public relations coup. And the pack at the back of the room lapped it up. Not one journalist challenged the facts and figures. How could they? No one, including me, had any real idea that what had been trundled into the boardroom was a load of bunk. We scribes were merely general reporters with little understanding of the immigration department and no inside sources.

At this particular meeting, Tory MP Jim Hawkes, then chairman of the standing committee, could hardly contain his enthusiasm for the program. He was so impressed by the statistics shovelled his way that he recommended the government "send a very clear signal to posts abroad that Canada needs jobs and is looking for their help in expanding the Entrepreneur Program. The clearest signal would be to raise the annual intake targets for entrepreneurs in 1986 to 5,000-7,000 and to 8,000-10,000 in 1987."

Then I had a little luck. I managed to snag a mid-level program officer whose voice bristled with frustration.

In other words, swing open the doors to these affluent foreigners and watch Canada prosper. The committee had caught the entrepreneurial fever, and the mandarins at the immigration department were applauded for a job well done. As I sat in a back row listening to all the hype, something made me feel uneasy. The presentation was just too slick, the bureaucrats too earnest and the mood too upbeat.

According to the colour-coded graphs on aluminum easels, 2,094 immigrant entrepreneurs were admitted to Canada in 1984, investing $817 million and creating 8,271 jobs. And since the program was first launched, more than 11,000 business immigrants had been granted landed status in Canada, investing $3.4 billion and creating almost 25,000 jobs in the process. Committee members were awed by these impressive figures, and I dutifully reported them like every other reporter covering the show, and like every other journalist who had covered the annual event since 1979.

But I had doubts, serious doubts, and it took a lot of earnest persuasion to convince my editor to cut me some slack to check them out. His prime concern was daily coverage. He felt uneasy about letting me go on "a wild-goose chase" and leaving the Hill manned by only five reporters. However, he finally relented, giving me a few hours a day to see what I could find out. That week I began calling immigration officials with one very simple request. I wanted to see the studies on which their impressive figures were based. My hunch that something was amiss was confirmed when my calls weren't returned. After almost two weeks of hounding, a communications officer with the department curtly informed me that the studies were stamped "Confidential." In other words, no Canadian citizen was allowed to see them.

I shot back sarcastically that the report surely wasn't a top-secret government document dealing with national security issues. So the public had a right to see it. I got no response.

I decided to sidestep the communications people and tore into the federal government's voluminous phone directory. I started calling civil servants in the department's program-development unit. Time and time again, I was referred to the communications branch. It was like listening to a mantra: "Call communications."

Then I had a little luck. I managed to snag a mid-level program officer whose voice bristled with frustration. He offered me a "backgrounder" on the proviso that I not quote or identify him. I agreed.

The figures so prominently highlighted before the parliamentary committee, he said, reflected "only the declared intention" of entrepreneurs. "We don't really know what they are doing."

Now the red lights were flashing. I knew then that this program warranted a hard look, starting with the initial entrepreneur application form and ending with the arrival of these so-called job creators in Canada. This was soon confirmed during an interview with Mendel Green, an immigration lawyer in Toronto who proffered this choice tidbit. He mused that with a well-written proposal a consultant or lawyer could "take a chimpanzee, dress him up in a business suit and just have him grunt and technically get him through [the immigration process]."

Lawyer after lawyer regaled me with a litany of stories of abuses. All spoke of the ease with which their slimier colleagues got prospective immigrants into the country without doing what was promised.

I reconnected with the program officer and told him about my conversations with the legal boys. This time he offered a little more, telling me about a highly sensitive report compiled by the immigration department that stripped the shine off the program. Needless to say, I was anxious to get my hands on it, and a few days later, a brown paper envelope arrived on my desk via Canada Post. It was a copy of the report.

The document confirmed my suspicions. In a random survey carried out over the summer months, immigration officials pulled 1,056 case files for review. But in the preliminary run-through, they couldn't find 395 of the entrepreneurs. Of the 661 who were located, 308 refused to take part. In all, only 353 entrepreneurs across the country, or 18.8 percent of the original random sample, were questioned, and from that group, the immigration department concluded that the program had an overall success rate of 77 percent.

Now I'm no math wizard, but even I knew this was stretching reality. In late December, I landed an interview with Walter McLean, then minister of state for immigration, to talk about the program. At his right sat Kirk Bell, then director general of policy and program development for the department. Like trained cockatoos, both boasted a whopping 77 percent success rate, proudly noting that the numbers were confirmed in a very recent analysis of the program. So you would think they would let me have a copy of the report. Nothing doing.

"It's not for public consumption," Bell intoned. When I asked how the success rate could be so high, given that roughly 40 percent of the entrepreneurs in the original random sample couldn't be found and that 308 of the remaining 661 refused to take part, I was confronted by startled and anxious stares.

The minister did some quick mental math and said, "Good question. I just got the first quasi-executive summary of the study and just had a preliminary briefing on the whole survey." Visibly annoyed, he tossed the ball over to Bell, who gave an impassioned defence of the findings.

"They are statistically valid," the director general insisted. "Statistically you can give a 77 percent success rate across the board." The director general steadfastly maintained there was no reason to believe those who could not be found or who did not respond were more or less successful than those who had participated in the survey. "They are to be considered the same. There is no reason, statistically, to believe otherwise."

Yet in the fine print, the study noted: "One must always be concerned with the potential bias that could be introduced as a result of systematic differences between those who do respond and those who do not."

I then offered up another interesting find highlighted in the confidential document that explained why so few respondents participated. The entrepreneur application forms filed at the department's regional offices did not bother, in all cases, to record the intended address of the person at the time of landing or admission to Canada. Nor were they updated to reflect changes of address as the person moved. My observations, though, were met with blank stares.

After I left the interview, I pulled out all the stops. It took hours of deliberate and tactful persuasion before I finally enlisted the cooperation of my immigration contact, convincing him to supply me with a series of files on what the department had stamped "successful entrepreneur applicants." I got my hands on 20 files. Each had forms filled out by a lawyer to the immigration department, stating that the business was up and running. But when I went looking for these 20 businesses, I couldn't find one. They were all bogus companies, existing only on paper.

Later, when I asked immigration officials if they physically checked to determine whether the company actually existed, I was told the department didn't have the manpower to do that. Their defence? "The forms were signed by lawyers, officers of the court. Why should they lie?"

My story made banner headlines in the *Globe and Mail.* And that afternoon, after some goading from Opposition members, an embarrassed immigration minister announced in the House of Commons that he had ordered an immediate tightening of the regulations governing the program.

This was not an earth-shattering expose, but it was important on many levels. It showed a key immigration program running amok. Here were rich immigrants coming into the country on lies and misrepresentations. Yet instead of plugging the loopholes, bureaucrats, giddy over the size of these people's bank accounts, escorted them to the front of the line. In the meantime, ordinary immigrants were forced to wait years before finding out whether they were selected in the Canadian immigration lottery sweepstakes. The story also showed how the pack on the Hill was totally ill-prepared to deal with the topics they were covering. For years they had been used (and continue to be used) by government bureaucrats who must have giggled with glee at how easy it was to dupe Canada's famed national reporting pool. The journalists were content to report the government offerings as fact and without question. The result was a sorely misinformed public.

Defiant Mohawks, massive warehouses filled with cases of Canadian smokes, and high-speed boats plying the waterway between the U.S.-Canada border made for great television.

If editors simply allowed their reporters to stop hopping from one mundane event to the next in homogeneous packs and let them roam untethered, politicians and bureaucrats would be reluctant to pull these kinds of bogus PR stunts. Yet in the real world of newspapers and TV news, image is paramount. Editors and news directors want their men and women up front reporting live from the Hill. It gives their news outlet currency. I maintain that if they really want to make an impact and gain notoriety and respect, they should let a few of their scribes loose to dig out more noteworthy stories.

One thing that has bothered me about reporting is how quickly editors want to assign you to something else. For them, the story you've just filed is old news once it hits the papers or airwaves. Their objective is the headline or the news flash. For the most part, editors aren't interested in allowing their reporters a moment to step back to examine what they've done and, more important, to see what they've missed. It's a process that can have significant results.

In 1992 I did a documentary for *the fifth estate* on cigarette smuggling. It wasn't one of my more difficult investigations, but it was a sound piece of journalism. Defiant Mohawks, massive warehouses filled with cases of Canadian smokes, and high-speed boats plying the waterway between the U.S.-Canada border made for great television. We managed to get access to a major Native smuggling operation on the Akwesasne reserve on the islands in the St. Lawrence Seaway between Cornwall, Ontario, and Messina, New York. Irate politicians and hamstrung Mounties had fingered the breached border crossing at Cornwall as the largest, single entry point of contraband cigarettes into Canada from the United States. The Mohawks had devised a way to beat the Canadian tax collector by purchasing duty-free cigarettes in the United States and selling them back in Canada at cut-rate prices.

It was a trying time for the federal government until our political leaders devised a typically made-in-Canada solution. It lowered the taxes on Canadian cigarettes and the smuggling abated.

However, *the fifth estate* documentary was anything but satisfying for my producer Julian Sher and me. We both knew that it was just too easy to wag an accusing finger at the Mohawks. We also knew that in order to fill these warehouses to the rafters with thousands of cases of Export A, the smugglers had to have high-level suppliers with connections in the executive suites of cigarette companies.

In late 1997, we got back onto the story after hearing of an RCMP–New York State undercover operation that busted most of the major smugglers on the reserve. The cops also netted the so-called smuggling kingpin, Larry Miller, who lives in Messina, just down the road from the American side of Akwesasne.

According to the police, all the key players were charged. Or were they? What was telling, I thought, was that not one tobacco company executive was among the arrested. All these warehouses jammed to the rafters with cigarette cases and not even a measly company salesman floundering in the net. Where did the police think the contraband came from?

We decided to go where no Mountie had dared tread before—straight into the executive suites of tobacco giant RJR-MacDonald. Why RJR? Because every week for almost three years, Larry Miller and the boys purchased trailer truckloads of its top brand, Export A. And the kind of volume that Miller was moving didn't simply fall off the back of an 18-wheeler truck. He had to have an inside connection. Our job was to prove it.

At this point, we had little more to go on than what we had a few years earlier. But I did get a crucial tip from a police source that Larry Miller had partied with RJR executives at a posh $1,000-a-day fishing lodge near Campbell River, British Columbia. Still, with no inside source in the gang or at RJR, our renewed investigation was soon spinning its wheels. I started looking more closely at the key players, searching for a lead or a weak link. My former Native contacts were still smarting over the original documentary and would have nothing to do with me. And the people at RJR-MacDonald refused to comment because the case was before the courts. But they pointed out that they were assisting the authorities by supplying them with sales records and bills of lading. I wondered how Miller would feel about that.

I reviewed the facts. Miller was charged. No tobacco executive was. Miller was on bail and tethered to an electronic ankle bracelet while his former associates at RJR walked free. Miller, from what the cops told me, held firmly to the old adage of honour among thieves. In other words, you don't rat on your confederates. The suits at RJR were cooperating with the police. I was certain Miller would bristle at the fact that his former fishing buddies were doing that.

In my mind, our entire investigation hinged on somehow convincing the smuggler to provide us with a road map of his dealings with RJR. I picked up the phone and called Larry Miller. My first question: "Did you catch any big ones at the fishing lodge?"

Over the next few months of digging and relentless prodding, I managed to link Miller directly to Les Thompson, the top sales manager in charge of sales for the entire American East Coast. But, more important, I connected him to Stan Smith, the executive vice president and chief operating officer of RJR-MacDonald in Toronto. I proved that Smith and Miller partied together on a number of occasions at the B.C. fishing lodge. And for some bizarre reason, those parties always seemed to end in adolescent food fights. I even landed glossy colour photographs of the chummy executive and smuggler, arm in arm, lathered in whipped cream and dripping cheap red wine.

I also linked Smith and various RJR salesmen to a number of clandestine meetings with Miller and his gang in Canada and the United States. For me, this was what the original investigation had lacked all along, and we were finally able to do it. But it could only have been done with the support of the executive and senior producers at *the fifth estate.* This was a story that took time, money and resources. There was no guarantee we would nail it down. But we were given the opportunity to try. And that was what we needed.

Sometimes when I look at how the news media routinely miss obvious stories, I can't help but shake my head and wonder. So many scandals that eventually surface were covered in warning signs, and yet the journalists covering those areas or beats were oblivious to them.

The stock market is one beat rife with scandal. But for the most part, it is covered by platoons of reporters who act more like cheerleaders in the heady world of stocks, bonds and pork-belly futures. So when word of a huge financial fraud breaks, we usually find it wasn't a business reporter behind it, but a quasi-investigative body set up to oversee the trade or some company with a vested interest in the outcome of a particular business venture.

No doubt the most embarrassing example of a blown opportunity for reporters to do even the most basic reporting is the Bre-X Gold stock fraud. It may well go down as the journalistic fumble of the 20th century!

Bre-X is a classic story about greed and failed journalism. It is also a story of incredible naïveté, and leading the pack of the gullible was a gaggle of stupefied financial reporters. It's the story about how good judgement became no judgement; how people got swept away by mass euphoria, fuelled almost entirely by the hype in the news media.

In light of the most basic facts, this was a company that demanded scrutiny from the outset. First, it was headed by a couple of questionable business types. Second, the shares shot up to incredible heights on the stock market with each unchallenged utterance by the duo about how much gold lay beneath the surface of some steamy jungle patch in Indonesia.

Bre-X is a classic story about greed and failed journalism.

I work on a very simple premise. In fact, every good journalist works on it. If it sounds too good to be true, it usually is. In this case, however, all the financial scribes could see was the glitter of gold.

In 1991 a Bre-X share was worth 25 cents on the stock exchange. In April 1995, the company issued a press release announcing its property in Busang was "excellent to become a major gold producer." The stock started to rocket, reaching $15 in August of that year when another press release touted that the property could produce 500,000 ounces of gold a year and "has the potential to be one of the top-producing gold mines in the world."

No reporter bothered to question the fact that another major gold company had explored the site years earlier and found no gold. This key piece of information was not hidden from the eyes of journalists. It was public knowledge and could have been found easily had someone bothered to look. The euphoria continued unchecked. Press release after press release was issued hyping the property, and the clueless newshounds lapped up each one without a quibble. The gold-deposit estimates soared from 70 million to 200 million ounces, worth a cool $70 billion!

Investors besieged their brokers' offices. Buy was the order of the day, and the stock continued its meteoric climb, hitting more than $200 by late May 1996, when the shares were split 10 to 1. At its peak, just after the split, the stock sold for $28.16, the equivalent of $281 in the old shares. Then in April and May 1996, an ominous flag snapped in the brisk breeze. Two of the principal shareholders, David Walsh, chairman and chief promoter of Bre-X, and John Felderhof, a geologist and the company's head of exploration, respectively sold $28 million and $22 million of their shares. The sale didn't even trigger a dingle from any alarm bell.

But, in retrospect, what is even more disturbing about the Bre-X fiasco is that no reporter questioned the fact that while the ore samples showed a lot of gold, they had been tested by laboratories hired by the company. There had been *no* independent gathering and testing of samples!

In early March 1997, a key Bre-X geologist plummeted to his death from a helicopter in Indonesia, in what was labelled a suicide. That scared some investors, but the price of the shares didn't collapse until the end of the month, when Freeport-McMoran Copper and Gold of New Orleans landed a small stake in the Busang property. It carried out its own tests on some core samples and reported that there was no gold worth mining. Stockholders who held their shares until Bre-X's drilling estimates were questioned lost more than $3 billion.

Bre-X underscores the sheer laziness of business reporters who didn't perform due diligence on behalf of their readers and viewers. But once the gold bar dropped, they were out there with backhoes running into one another in a pathetic attempt to dig up a scoop. Like a bunch of crazed hyenas, they leaped off the Bre-X bandwagon and onto the book writers' gravy train. The subsequent "investigative stories" and books could wallpaper a small town.

When I'm invited to speak to journalism students, or even working reporters, about what I do, I always get the feeling that they are looking for some kind of magic formula on how to break the big story. There is a formula, but there is no magic.

There are a number of factors that go into the making of a good investigative reporter. The main two are motivation and a finely honed sixth sense that beeps when you're onto a good story and buzzes when the lies start flying.

Another important attribute is the ability to listen hard to what people are saying and not dismiss them outright because their claims sound farfetched. So often I've latched onto incredible stories that other reporters had tossed off as too unbelievable to be true. Well, they turned out to be true, and they made for amazing headlines and riveting documentaries.

Nothing annoys me more than hearing a reporter state with know-it-all arrogance that because the police arrested a suspect, he must be guilty. Tell that to Guy Paul Morin, Donald Marshall and David Milgaard, all wrongfully charged and later convicted of murder. From the outset, their cases were fraught with inconsistencies largely due to sloppy police investigations deliberately orchestrated with one aim in mind: to win a guilty verdict. Most reporters bought the police news releases hook, line and sinker. They never thought for a moment there might be another side to the story—the side of the accused. All they had to do was seek and listen. I've learned one important fact about listening, and that is whatever you're told, it either has the ring of truth or the static of lies. All it takes is a little time and effort to get at the truth.

Motivation and perseverance carry a reporter through an investigation.

They are the keys to developing forthright contacts and well-placed sources and require working the telephone into the night and chasing interminable paper trails. Most of all, an investigative reporter's job isn't nine-to-five. It takes a special breed of reporter to do investigative work. Some have been likened to crusaders defending the victim and the underdog, others to ego-driven diggers with a zeal for exposing scandals. Whatever the reason, what is paramount is getting at the truth and reporting it.

The role of all journalists is to question and challenge. It is to provide accurate and solid information so that the public can make informed decisions about the community in which they live. The role of investigative journalists is to ensure this happens.

The reality is that the news media are probably the most powerful of all our institutions today. We have a responsibility and an obligation to inform our readers, listeners and viewers, and any attempt to stop reporters from carrying out investigations is an abdication of our responsibility.

Politicians, Journalists and the Need for Civil Dialogue

The press has become the most powerful force in Western countries. It has surpassed in power the executive, legislative, and judiciary.
—Aleksandr Solzhenitsyn, Harvard University, June 1978

SHOULD THE RELATIONSHIP of a reporter to a politician be "as a dog to a pole"? Claire Hoy, longtime member of the Ottawa press gallery, once suggested as much. And judging by some of the political journalism practised in this country, he is not the only member of the media to think so. But the increasing cynicism and distrust felt by Canadians—for both politicians and journalists—suggests that democracy is ill-served by a urination model of political news reporting.

An erosion of faith in public life and those who participate in political processes is one of the dominant trends of our time. How can it be explained? Are politicians markedly less capable and less honest today than they were a generation ago? Are there more genuine scandals and conflicts of interest now than there used to be? Or are there other possible explanations? These are questions that seem increasingly to be on the minds of disgruntled politicians and disenchanted citizens alike.

Moreover, the influence wielded by journalists and the news media appears to have increased significantly in the years since Solzhenitsyn's observation noted above. At the same time, politicians seem much less able to exercise authority today than in generations past.

One of the authors of this essay has a personal basis for comparison, having served a term as a member of British Columbia's legislative assembly. Upon returning to private life, he provided regular political commentary and analysis through a weekly newspaper column and frequent radio and television appearances. He experienced a much greater ability to influence public opinion and policy from within the ranks of the media than he did from within the legislature.

Other politicians have left office under a cloud of manufactured "scandal," only to be proven innocent of the accusations against them once out of office.

The media time and space devoted to their vindication, however, is never remotely as significant as the attention given the stories that once condemned them.

This tendency is disturbing for those who hold the tenets of democracy dear, believing in the importance of a political process by which representatives making decisions on the behalf of citizens are scrutinized and elected by a majority of voters. On the other hand, the backgrounds and opinions of journalists and their editors rarely undergo any similar examination; in fact, their organizations are, for the most part, unaccountable.

The tendencies to emphasize drama, conflict and personalities over in-depth discussions of policies and their implications are easily identified in the coverage of virtually every federal and provincial election campaign of the past generation.

Canada's Royal Commission on Newspapers noted in 1981 that Canadians by and large believe that the news media "have responsibilities to the public different from those of other businesses." Moreover, news consumers who recognize the extent to which democratic decisions are heavily influenced by mediated information increasingly believe that those responsibilities extend beyond news organizations to working journalists themselves.

Bill Deedes, a former editor of London, England's *Daily Telegraph*, suggested in 1993 that reporters had moved from subservience in the 1930s, to equality in the 1950s, to superiority today. Not unreasonably, Canadian citizens expect the news media to play a responsible role in maintaining our democratic institutions. This necessarily involves reflecting the diverse perspectives of the communities being served; providing objective information about public issues (or at least acknowledging that objectivity is not possible in the selection and repackaging process); clarifying the choices embodied in those issues; and encouraging people's active participation in decision-making processes that affect them.

It is difficult to identify a Canadian news organization today that comes close to meeting such expectations. In fact, the news biases documented by communications analysts are nowhere so evident as in political reporting. The tendencies to emphasize drama, conflict and personalities over in-depth discussions of policies and their implications are easily identified in the coverage of virtually every federal and provincial election campaign of the past generation. Given the competitive commercial imperatives of most news media, requiring them to deliver audiences to their advertisers, and so ensure that they entertain as well as inform, the extent to which politics has become a kind of modern-day blood sport is probably not so surprising.

But it is regrettable. The above factors, coupled with the constraints of time and space, and the man-bites-dog phenomenon that justifies focusing attention on the aberrant, as opposed to the more common, necessarily highlights negative news of a confrontational nature. The conflict bias is so entrenched that political leaders who have favoured a consultative, cooperative form of leadership are often criticized for their style, or simply ignored because of it.

Furthermore, media coverage of government policy announcements that may contain specific information about legislation or programs of interest to the public often ends up focusing on someone's negative reaction to the announcement, while excluding details relevant to the public. Budget-day stories have provided classic illustrations of this inclination, allowing the critical perspectives of opposition members and special-interest groups to shape the coverage at the expense of the budget particulars.

Nor is the negativity confined to government initiatives or governing party representatives. Recent coverage of federal Reform party leader Preston Manning caused one disgruntled reader of the *Vancouver Sun* to suggest in a letter to the editor that "If Mr. Manning were to walk on water, the *Sun*'s headline next day would be: 'Reform leader can't swim.'"

The amount and nature of mediation that occurs in political journalism has often been criticized in the context of the diminishing sound bite. One U.S. study determined that the average length of a TV clip featuring a politician speaking directly shrank from 42 seconds in 1968 to less than 10 seconds in 1992. This trend, which has been duplicated in Canadian political coverage, invariably results in greater emphasis on journalists' interpretation and analysis. In fact, it is now increasingly common for television coverage of politicians to feature no sound bite at all; instead, an image of the political figure is used as a visual backdrop to the explanatory observations of a reporter or critic.

Television's widely acknowledged dominance in the context of election coverage, in particular, means that the availability of interesting visual material has a disproportionate influence on what is considered newsworthy. This development, in combination with the tendency to focus on the personal style of leaders—as opposed to the likely impact of policies—can have serious consequences.

Even relatively benign incidents can undermine a politician's credibility. During the 1996 federal election, Bloc Québécois leader Gilles Duceppe toured a cheese factory wearing a hygienic cap that is required attire in most food-service operations. He looked about as silly as anyone does in a plastic shower cap. Television stations across the country aired the footage of Duceppe repeatedly, making him appear clownish in one of his first campaign appearances. Amazingly a national political columnist defended the television emphasis, arguing that the manufactured embarrassment actually helped voters to make responsible choices.

It is one thing for the satirical CBC-TV comedy program *This Hour Has 22 Minutes* to lampoon politics and politicians, but when a senior Canadian journalist in a respected national news publication referred to Prime Minister Kim Campbell as "Woody Allen in drag," what enlightenment did he offer? Has the entertainment imperative infected the news to such an extent that creating an evocative image or coining a quotable insult have now become the raison d'être of even mainstream political reporting?

The sneering, disrespectful tone of most political journalism today is as disturbing as its substance, which seems to consist of a combination of character assassination and skullduggery. Imagine if other branches of journalism—business or sports, for instance—were similarly infected by the kind of Frank magazine–inspired manner currently reserved for politics. We might read business stories written along the lines of the following fictitious example:

> Molson Breweries, in a blatant attempt to increase profits, announced today that it had developed a beer with a two-percent-increased alcohol content, which will be sold for only pennies more than standard brands. Cagey about the gains being made by industry competitors, and concerned about recent criticisms of its questionable advertising appeals to underage drinkers, the company's motives in launching this new product are being seriously questioned. One industry insider commented: "Molson's is making a cynical play for the pocketbooks of some of society's most vulnerable. They're going after alcoholics, plain and simple."

The mainstream business press in North America would be unlikely to carry such a story. At least not yet. That's not to say the relentless negativism of political journalism isn't already spilling over into news media generally. It is difficult to ignore, for instance, that negative news usually leads most newscasts or covers the front pages of newspapers. Meanwhile, good news is almost always relegated to secondary status.

Political journalists have long led the way in this corrosive brand of reporting. Ever since the Watergate scandal of the 1970s, ambitious American reporters and their editors seem to dream of destroying presidents. In Canada, as well, our media analysis of politics often consists of a rush to judgement based on anonymous sources and an assumption of Machiavellian motives.

Parliamentary press galleries are symptomatic of these biases and a kind of "Watergate envy." The pack journalism that prevails in Ottawa and most provincial capitals only too rarely provides original or thoughtful reporting; rather, the various media outlets represented are under intense pressure to cover the collectively designated "scandal of the day." And this is done through reporting almost exclusively on question period—which is hardly representative of the work or essence of our parliamentary institutions—or in "scrums" of politicians, who often appear on television screens as caged animals being baited mercilessly by shouting, disrespectful reporters.

A couple of years ago an article provocatively entitled "Why Americans Hate the Media" graced the cover of the *Atlantic Monthly.* Its author, James Fallows, at the time an editor of the magazine, was not criticizing Hollywood's violence or Madison Avenue's advertising ethics. His focus was largely on the U.S. media's coverage of public affairs.

Ever since the Watergate scandal of the 1970s, ambitious American reporters and their editors seem to dream of destroying presidents.

Fallows's critique—expanded on in his 1996 book *Breaking the News: How the Media Undermine American Democracy*—documents the significant discrepancy between the aspects of political discourse emphasized by the news media and what voters actually care about. Journalists, he argues, tend to be political junkies, interested in the political process, with its attendant party intrigues and campaign strategies. In contrast, the majority of news consumers are more concerned about how politics affects their daily lives, and less interested in the soap opera of backroom politics.

Reviewing the kinds of questions asked of politicians by reporters and by ordinary citizens, Fallows concludes that the media inevitably focus on the "how" of politics: "How will you defeat your opponent? How will you respond to the accusations?" Voters, on the other hand, want to know about the "what" of policy: "What is your position on universal health care? What will you do to reduce my taxes?"

Of course, journalists' myopic emphasis on the style of politics over the substance of policies has been aided and abetted by politicians themselves, most of whom are, after all, media junkies. The incestuousness of this relationship, in which both journalists and politicians need each other and feed—as well as feed off—the other's weaknesses, is clearly part of the problem. But if politics was covered more responsibly in the first place, and if the policy makers had some confidence that substantive issues would receive more attention, and hairstyles and personal ambitions less, they might abandon their reliance on the gimmickry of "spin doctors" and "pseudo events" to manipulate the media.

Nevertheless, criticizing the news media's performance publicly is a fool's game that most politicians realize they can't win. "Don't blame the messenger" may have been coined to remind the recipients of bad news that those who simply relay unfortunate information are hardly responsible for it, but it's been appropriated by the news media to excuse them from responsibility for a host of ills that they do, in fact, have some control over.

Moreover, this rationalization reinforces the notion that mediating information is a transparent process, involving simply the collection of data and its dissemination. This myth is reflected in the statement made by Canada's most trusted news anchor on a nightly basis. "And that's the kind of day it's been here at *CTV News*," intones Lloyd Robertson at the end of each newscast, obscuring the agenda-setting exercise involved.

Canadian newsroom editors have been known to attempt to inspire their investigative-reporting teams by extolling the virtues of certain U.S. news organizations.

Because, of course, "that" is just the day that CTV has chosen to share with its viewers. "That" is the product of an intense selection process replicated by all TV news organizations, which identifies a dozen stories out of hundreds, a few interview subjects out of thousands, while posing particular questions, selecting particular images and packaging particular sound bites in a tightly scripted program designed to entertain as much—or more—as inform.

And as many others have pointed out, the biases inherent in such a selection process—whether or not they are conscious—necessarily determine, if not what we think, then at the very least what we think about, not to mention the importance we attach to top-of-the-news or front-page stories, relative to those buried someplace closer to the weather reports.

This agenda-setting capacity is particularly troubling in light of a peculiar aspect of our system of government: the phenomenon whereby opposition members of our parliaments and legislatures regularly seem to take delight in what is essentially bad news for their country or province. And the close working alliance between opposition members and the journalists who report on government activities is such that the news media appear to have adopted a mock-celebratory tone whenever misfortune strikes. When unemployment rates go up or environmental disaster occurs, oppositionists and reporters seem to rub their hands in glee over the inescapable conclusion (to them at least) that the destruction can—and will—be blamed on the supposed ineptitude of the government.

Indeed, the more experienced, and usually more jaded of political reporters, appear to have spent so many years immersed in an environment reliant on the "us and them," win-lose nature of partisan politics that many manifest an unconscious and indiscriminate "let's bring down the government" attitude.

Canadian newsroom editors have been known to attempt to inspire their investigative-reporting teams by extolling the virtues of certain U.S. news organizations. Apparently forcing the resignation of politicians represents the pinnacle of success in the view of some senior news staff. In a similar vein, listening in on press-gallery chatter prior to a government news conference or political scrum, one might be excused for mistaking the participants for members of a police sting operation.

One particularly instructive case involved Mike Harcourt, former premier of British Columbia. Widely described by journalists as being "too nice" and "too honest" for his job, Harcourt resigned over a scandal that erupted around the inappropriate use of charity bingo funds by a former executive of the New Democratic Party, well before Harcourt's tenure. Although all the evidence was clear about the premier's complete lack of involvement in or knowledge of the issue, one TV reporter, upon learning a particular piece of information about the case, was overheard confiding to a colleague: "We're going to fucking nail Harcourt."

Is the democratic process served by these practices?

In 1996 the *Washington Post* printed the following comments:

> A few years ago, First Lady, Hillary Clinton, in the wake of the suicide of a U.S. navy admiral who had been under intense media scrutiny over his wearing of two medals, observed that "we now live in an evidence-free world." She lamented the circumstances which permit a lie to travel "halfway around the world before the truth can get out of someone's mouth," and

suggested that in such an environment, "people are reluctant to believe anything or anybody."

Throughout the 1990s, public opinion polls conducted by both Gallup and Angus Reid determined that only a small minority of Canadians (between four and 13 percent, depending on the survey) expressed strong confidence in and respect for the country's politicians. (For context, doctors were rated as high or very high in terms of their honesty and ethics by between 48 and 57 percent of poll respondents.)

These attitudes have shifted significantly over time. Consider that in 1979, 38 percent of Canadians surveyed indicated they had "a great deal" or "quite a lot" of respect and confidence in the House of Commons. By 1995 the number had dropped to 19 percent.

Interestingly enough, the same polls revealed that respect for journalists is also declining and appears to be at an all-time low. Reporters were accorded close to bottom-feeder status, earning the confidence of between 15 and 25 percent of those surveyed, suggesting that Canadians see them as only marginally more trustworthy than lawyers or, indeed, the politicians they regularly slag.

The future of our democracy depends on responsible and ethical people who effectively represent the diversity of perspectives and experiences within the broader population.

The plummeting reputations of both elected officials and those who report on their activities is no coincidence. If journalists are regularly seen by the general public to be subverting or expressing contempt for politics, that can't help but influence public attitudes about participants in the process, including the journalists themselves. It seems that the public has, in some respects, decided to shoot the messenger. James Fallows, in *Breaking the News,* even goes as far as to claim a direct link between the high levels of cynicism and declining newspaper readership and rampant channel surfing among previously dedicated news viewers.

Among the regrettable consequences of today's pervasive characterization of politics as a cesspool is the extent to which it is becoming more and more difficult to recruit good people for public office. Not surprisingly, the "politician as scumbag" rhetoric appears to have become a self-fulfilling prophecy, so much so that individuals motivated by a public-service ethic no longer identify with politics as a reputable profession. Channelling their energies in different directions instead, they arguably leave the field open to people with less noble and more ego-driven or opportunistic motivations.

Moreover, as long as politics is defined by the media as a macho contest requiring a willingness to go for the jugular, it will continue to be especially difficult to recruit not just honest and consensus-seeking men, but competent and committed women, who are still socialized to value cooperation over confrontation. The future of our democracy depends on responsible and ethical people who effectively represent the diversity of perspectives and experiences within the broader population. The sought-after goal of a more equitable parliament is made even more elusive by the current media environment.

Furthermore, our long-standing presumption that a democratic election process guarantees our freedom is seriously suspect in light of the contemporary news coverage of politics. Since the process by which voters access information is biased, and the information about those seeking office, and/or governing on our behalf, is tainted, the process can't really be considered fair and democratic.

In the United States, where many of the destructive media practices discussed here have been exercised excessively for a much longer period of time, only a third of eligible voters bother to vote in federal elections. In fact, some recent American research suggests that confrontational political advertising campaigns have a negative impact on the number of those who vote, and some strategists have confessed that such campaigns are part of a deliberate strategy to "shrink the electorate" by forcing a lower voter turnout. Of course, there are many other factors at play beyond the media coverage, but it is troubling to consider what impact Canada's own increasingly negative news environment may have for voter turnout, which has been slowly but steadily declining in recent years.

Critics of the status quo might be forgiven for entertaining themselves by imagining the following: a capital city in which the members of the press gallery expand their attention to Parliament beyond the partisan antics and scandal mongering of question period to sometimes report on the more substantive debates about policies, which occasionally illuminate their implications for citizens; a country where radio talk-show hosts abandon their often deliberately inflammatory rhetoric to pursue more frequently genuine interviews that actually explore the complexities of issues rather than dwell on superficialities; a world in which journalists in general exercise healthy skepticism and undertake in-depth investigations devoid of malicious intent and without actively seeking to "make" their careers by destroying the reputation of someone else in the process.

Are we dreaming in Technicolor? Are these fantasies fundamentally at odds with human nature? Or is it possible to construct a new form of political journalism in which the limitations of our present system and its entrenched practices are recognized and rejected as counterproductive to the goals of participatory democracy?

Most reporters—particularly those new to the profession—would take issue with British journalist Rebecca West's definition of journalism as being essentially "an ability to meet the challenge of filling the space." And those in the business of training journalists to fulfill their mediating role most certainly see their task as one that goes far beyond giving reporters the tools necessary to "fill space." In order to ensure that citizens reliant on journalists place more trust in the products of their efforts, however, a few changes to journalism education are doubtless necessary.

In recent years, as the structure and ownership of Canadian newspapers has become more monopolistic, there appears to have been a corresponding decline in reporters with in-depth knowledge of particular areas of expertise.

One of these involves the importance of ensuring that those interpreting the world have some experience in that world that goes beyond journalism school and the acquisition of practical reporting techniques. Despite the current trend in higher education of focusing on applied skills, the journalism profession, in particular, begs a broader education. Aspiring journalists should be taught not only how to research and write stories, but also how to think critically, value and integrate diverse perspectives and historical context, and be aware of and work to overcome the complex biases inherent in their jobs.

To this end, obtaining a degree in another discipline—whether in arts or sciences—prior to pursuing journalism training is valuable. Having work experience outside the news media is also advisable, in order to gain an appreciation for the contexts within which mediated news information is received and used. Knowledge and experience gained in these ways contribute to a more complex and textured understanding and analysis of issues, which seems likely to result in more comprehensive and responsible reporting.

Building on "real world" experiences by undertaking a one- or two-year journalism program at the graduate level after having pursued another discipline and gained work experience in another environment would appear to combine the best of both worlds. In contrast, providing technical instruction in the arts of researching, interviewing, writing and/or broadcasting information seems woefully inadequate preparation for dealing with the multifaceted task of making sense of the world on behalf of others.

At the same time, arguments over the relative merits of generalists and specialists in the journalism profession miss the point: we need both. We need generalists whose broad understanding of trends can help readers, listeners and viewers make sense of the big picture, and we need specialists who bring to their interpretative duties a detailed enough background to be able to ask the kind of informed questions that would never occur to their generalist colleagues or the public itself.

In recent years, as the structure and ownership of Canadian newspapers has become more monopolistic, there appears to have been a corresponding decline in reporters with in-depth knowledge of particular areas of expertise. This trend, driven by economies of scale, is as unfortunate as what appears to be a concomitant decline in diversity of perspectives, particularly in regional and ideological terms. Journalism schools should both recognize these realities and encourage discussion among students about the impact such trends are likely to have on their profession and its ability to fulfill the expectations placed on it in a pluralistic, democratic society.

Another aspect of journalism training that could make a difference to our political coverage is the attention paid to interview techniques. In addition to acknowledging the problems identified by James Fallows, and working to ask questions that relate to the "what" of policies, instead of the "how" of partisan strategies, journalists would do well to consider the advice of John Sawatsky.

Considered one of the best investigative journalists in Canada, Sawatsky goes out of his way not to ask tough-sounding, leading or accusatory questions, which he claims actually repress information. The effectiveness of his approach is evident in his work—for example, in his book *Mulroney: The Politics of Ambition,* in which he revealed a great deal of previously unknown but telling information about the former prime minister's career.

Sawatsky attributes his success to assuming a neutral approach, avoiding sensationally charged words and asking open-ended or so-called "dumb" questions. Based on his years of direct experience, and the research he has conducted in his capacity as a longtime journalism instructor at Ottawa's Carleton University, he has discovered that assuming the stance of curious child, rather than an aggressive attorney, actually elicits much more revealing responses.

This technique in no way advocates a return to the days when the relationship between politicians and reporters could be described in terms of a chummy old boys' network. But surely if the goal of political reporting is to serve the public by unearthing information of relevance, it makes sense to adopt an interview approach that recognizes the answers, not the implications embodied in leading questions, are the important thing.

Research also suggests that people are less likely to condemn politicians when they are asked questions that require them to think about real, tangible problems. Somehow the very process of engaging an elected official in a search for pragmatic solutions encourages media consumers themselves to consider the challenges of the specific issue under discussion. Whether you label this "public journalism" or common sense, it seems a much more productive approach than unabashed muckraking or character assassination.

Writing in the *Canadian Parliamentary Review* in 1994, prior to entering federal politics, Stéphane Dion, now minister of intergovernmental relations, suggested that editorial writers and columnists should do more than criticize politicians and policies: they should actually be required to suggest viable alternatives or frankly admit that they themselves can't think of any concrete solutions. This practice alone would go a long way toward tempering the destructive condemnation that does little to contribute to either our understanding of issues or our ability to solve problems.

When veteran American newsman Walter Lippmann declared in 1920 that "There can be no liberty for a community which lacks the means by which to detect lies," he was arguing in favour of the need for a well-trained news media ready to serve the public interest. Nearly 80 years and several technological revolutions later, an equally compelling case can be made for the importance of a well-trained public able to appreciate that mediated information, by its nature, incorporates layers and layers of "lies," albeit mostly inadvertent.

The phenomenon observed in the United States recently, whereby President Bill Clinton's approval rating seemed unaffected—or indeed buoyed—by the media's feeding frenzy around his alleged illicit relationship with Monica Lewinsky, led many to conclude that public appetites and attitudes may not be remotely reflected by the priorities of the news media.

Indeed, attitudes about media excesses on both sides of the U.S.-Canada border would seem to give weight to James Fallows's argument about the need for political reporters to refocus on issues that actually affect the general public. Whatever our desire to be titillated, is it possible that our instinct for self-preservation—and all that that implies—is stronger?

As we head into a new century, and the challenges involved in governing become increasingly demanding and complex, it is more important than ever that we attract the best people possible to public service, and ensure that their activities on our behalf are scrutinized and reported on as fully and fairly as possible.

In the context of intensifying calls for political reform, it is more than reasonable to request journalistic reform, as well. As citizens reach for new ways of governing, and yearn for new methods of community participation, the news media have the ability to provide needed leadership. This will necessarily involve a suspension of cynicism and a willingness to experiment with some new, more constructive approaches to the coverage of politics.

We hope the fourth estate is up to the task. Our democracy may depend on it.

IAN HANOMANSING

Ian Hanomansing is a national reporter for CBC-TV and the host of Newsworld's *Pacific Rim Report.* He is also a substitute anchor for CBC-TV's *The National* and *Sunday Report.*

Born in Port of Spain, Trinidad, Hanomansing grew up in Sackville, New Brunswick. He received a bachelor of arts from Mount Allison University in Sackville, with majors in political science and sociology. He also has a bachelor of laws degree from Dalhousie University in Halifax.

Hanomansing worked at radio stations in Moncton, New Brunswick, and Amherst and Halifax in Nova Scotia before joining CBC-TV in Halifax in 1986. His news assignments have included the *Exxon Valdez* oil spill and San Francisco earthquake in 1989; the Los Angeles riots in 1992; the Vancouver Stanley Cup riot in 1994; the Atlanta Summer Olympics in 1996; the handover of Hong Kong to China in 1997; and the 1998 Winter Olympics in Nagano, Japan. He has a particular interest in legal issues and has covered numerous court cases, including the criminal trials of former B.C. premiers Bill Bennett and Bill Vander Zalm.

Courtroom Cameras and the Right to See Justice Done

Court is a fascinating place. As a reporter, I have had the privilege of being paid to watch portions of dozens of court cases. I have seen an accused murderer's knees sag as he heard a jury declare him guilty. I have watched a lawyer's cross-examination shatter the credibility of a witness. I have heard both eloquent judges and boorish judges. Through it all, I have wished that I could use the basic tool of my trade, the television camera, to show it all. Anyone, of course, can go and watch court proceedings firsthand. But although many people have a great interest in what happens in court, they don't always have the opportunity to exercise their right to be there.

That is why I passionately believe in the importance of getting cameras into court. For years I and many of my colleagues have argued publicly and privately for this opportunity. In response we have heard the same argument over and over again: it would distort the process. Lawyers would play to the camera, witnesses would be intimidated, juries would be unduly influenced, and video footage would be used out of context.

What strikes me as particularly ironic about the opposition of certain lawyers to cameras in the courtroom is the fact that these same lawyers, who usually rely on a painstaking review of the facts to support their cases, make their anticamera arguments without a shred of evidence, though many are quick to point to the spectacle of the O. J. Simpson trial. A trial that happened in a different country. A trial that, even by American standards, attracted an unusual degree of media and public attention. A trial where the most outrageous element—for most people—was a verdict delivered by jurors who were sequestered and never saw any of the media coverage until after they found Simpson not guilty.

Needless to say, the Simpson trial has stiffened the resolve of the opponents of cameras in the courtroom. But let's move on. Reporters like myself are willing to make a significant concession and forget about televising trials. But that doesn't mean we have to abandon the cause of cameras in the courtroom altogether. Instead, the time has come for journalists, lawyers, judges and the public to turn the debate to other court proceedings that are less sensitive and don't raise the same issues.

First appearances are a case in point. They usually last just a couple of minutes. The accused shuffles into court and a date is quickly set for dealing with matters like bail. There is no evidence presented. No witnesses. No jury. Even the most flamboyant lawyer would be hard-pressed to play to a camera here.

Watching a judge sternly explain why someone is being sent to jail can be a sobering experience.

But sometimes the public has a great interest in seeing the person accused of a crime that has, in some way, touched the community. I have been in many courtrooms that have been filled to overflowing with people who needed to see this small part of the judicial process.

For those who were equally interested but unable to get to court, a single, stationary camera could record without intruding on or affecting the proceedings in any way. How is justice possibly better served by the status quo in which we rely on a hastily drawn sketch or a picture from a camera pressed against a police car window?

Then there is the act of sentencing. Watching a judge sternly explain why someone is being sent to jail can be a sobering experience. And so it should be. After all, one of the fundamental goals of sentencing is something called general deterrence: discouraging members of the public from committing the same crime. But the vast majority of people will never see a sentence being handed down. Instead, the sentence is explained in a few words in a newspaper or in a line of narration on television.

If ever there was something the legal community should strive to televise, this is it! There is no jury and no witnesses. Even the lawyers have stopped talking. The verdict is in, so there is no trial that could somehow be prejudiced. The judge's reasons have been researched and are usually written down. What harm could possibly be done by the camera?

When it comes to appeals, too, there is no jury to worry about. There are no witnesses and no evidence is introduced. The verdict has been rendered.

What remains is a discussion of legal issues among lawyers and judges. And quite often the very fact that a verdict is being appealed means that those legal issues are significant.

So, once again, how exactly is justice served by limiting reporters to sketches to show what happens inside the courtroom during an appeal? Indeed, there is no doubt that a television story is much easier to understand when the viewer can see what is being talked about and hear what is being said.

However, that brings me to what opponents of courtroom cameras would consider the Achilles' heel of my proposals: give reporters video of a court proceeding and inevitably, whether through bad faith or sheer incompetence, the video will be used out of context.

I have heard this contention from judges, lawyers and members of the public, and it is time to put it to rest. In fact, it is an argument for broad censorship. If reporters are so fallible, why stop at restrictions on cameras in court? Why not bring in widespread bans on many court proceedings until the last appeal is extinguished? In fact, that would solve many so-called "problems." No doubt many accused people, as well as witnesses and lawyers, would prefer there be no coverage at all of the trials they are involved in.

So, once again, how exactly is justice served by limiting reporters to sketches to show what happens inside the courtroom during an appeal?

Fortunately this matter was firmly resolved long ago. For more than a century, judges in Canada have recognized the importance of public scrutiny. They clearly knew such scrutiny would come at a cost. Sometimes the media accounts would cause discomfort. Sometimes they would be wrong. But it was crucial that justice not be done in secret. Secrecy breeds rumours and corrodes confidence. It allows those who do badly to go unpunished and lets those who do well go unnoticed.

We have all heard the lofty sentiment that justice must not only be done, but must also be seen to be done. But many critics of courtroom cameras seem unable to make the connection between that sentiment and the fact that the camera allows a lot more people to take a look.

Frankly I think the reason for such blindness is that many people in the legal community feel the less media coverage the better. I see this whenever I go to court. It begins at the door to every courthouse in British Columbia that has a sign that reads: No Knives, Guns, Cameras or Recording Devices.

The antimedia sentiment continues inside the courtroom. Many lawyers won't talk to reporters even if it is simply a case of helping us better understand what is going on. I remember pleading with one prominent government lawyer to explain to me whether a particular proceeding was a constitutional reference or a hearing or something else. He politely but firmly told me: "I do my talking in court."

Mark my words: open the courtroom door to cameras and many journalists will use that access to enlighten their audience. Making news stories easier to understand is just the beginning. Documentary producers will use the footage to explore legal issues. Teachers and professors would be able to show their students Canadian lawyers and judges in action.

Still, the door has opened slightly. The Supreme Court of Canada currently allows cameras to record and broadcast some of its sessions. The footage has been used in news stories and has even been broadcast live without causing the roof of the Supreme Court to collapse or lawyers to abandon their carefully written submissions to look directly into the camera and begin to dance. But I do know people who eagerly tuned in to see, for the first time, the highest court of the country in full swing.

The time has come to follow this Supreme Court precedent. If the refusal to put cameras in courtrooms has truly been rooted in concern for witnesses, lawyers and juries, there should be little opposition to videotaping first appearances, sentencing and appeals. If there are other, unspoken reasons against using cameras in such proceedings, let's hear them.

It will also be a challenge for the media. We must use this opportunity to prove the importance of our role in the judicial process; show that we aren't merely interested in the tawdry, sensational cases; and explain and scrutinize the court with fairness and intelligence.

I can't wait!

TRINA MCQUEEN

Trina McQueen is president of Discovery Channel, one of Canada's top-ranked television specialty channels. Active in professional and community activities, she is a board member of the Banff Television Foundation, the World Wildlife Fund and the Canadian Journalism Foundation.

She chairs the Action Group on Violence in Television, a broadcast industry group developing a classification system for Canadian television, and is a member of the advisory boards of the University of Waterloo, Carleton University and the School of Journalism at Ryerson University. In 1995 she was granted an honorary doctoral degree from Mount St. Vincent University, and for eight years served on the board of Toronto's Canadian Stage Company.

Before joining Discovery Channel, McQueen enjoyed a 25-year career with the CBC. Beginning as an on-air reporter and program host, she later held senior management positions in journalism, entertainment programming, advertising sales and business operations. She was vice president of television news, current affairs and Newsworld from 1988 to 1992.

No Good and Evil Please, We're Journalists

A POLITICAL COLUMNIST once said that it is difficult to write about "journalistic ethics" without sounding like a jerk. I am going to write not only about journalistic ethics, but also about journalism on the subject of ethics. Surely this is double jerkishness. Nevertheless, I will carry on, and you have been warned.

Journalism about ethics reminds me of those "thin book" jokes. There isn't much of it. Even when an event seems to have a moral centre, journalists will report around, over, under and through the moral issue. One case in point: the 1998 controversy over providing financial aid to people who had contracted Hepatitis C from tainted blood. The controversy was hugely reported, not just in column inches but in column acreage. The facts of the matter were well documented. There was extensive background analysis of surrounding issues. Among the issues explained and debated were the political clout of Health Minister Allan Rock within cabinet and his chances of becoming prime minister; the use of the whip to force Liberals to vote with the government; federal-provincial clashes; and the personalities and influences of the various lobby groups.

What got very little ink and airtime were the principles that a society might use in deciding whether compensation was justified. Much was made of the tears streaming down the face of a dissident Liberal who voted with the government. But how had she come to her original decision that compensation was a moral duty? And how had she balanced those principles against the principles used in deciding her political duty? In mainstream journalism, the moral issues were mostly edited out. Or, more likely, they weren't even there to be edited.

But before we consider what's left out of premillennium journalism, let's consider what is lately there: the Stars. Princess Diana, Bill Clinton, Margaret Trudeau, O. J. Simpson, Mr. and Mrs. Matthew Barrett, Pamela Anderson. Beautiful, rich and sensational, these characters and their like are redolent of power and sexuality; and all are beset by extremely interesting personal demons.

Many academics and journalists wonder why there is so much in newspapers, magazines and television about these folks and so little about the

Chiapas revolt in Mexico or hydroelectric restructuring in North America. No, honestly, they really do. They argue about it at conferences; they write books and columns and theses. It's called the "tabloidization of news." Some of this tabloidization is wild rumour and some of it is outright lies. It is a truth universally acknowledged that this is deplorable. It is also generally agreed that some tabloid journalism is true but, in any case, there is too much of it; and too much, as Butterfly (no relation) McQueen said "just ain't fitten."

As we enter the new millennium, tabloid journalism may have reached terminal velocity. For example, the next American president cannot reasonably be expected to provide the wealth of embarrassingly riveting intimate material that the current one does. Some standards cannot be matched. Yet we can predict that attempts will be made and that the coverage of them will be exuberant.

The characters in hot stuff are truly characters: the demonic killers, the fabulous babes, the hot commander in chief and the angelic princess.

What distresses some earnest media thinkers about tabloid news is that it fits uncomfortably into the usually accepted noble purposes of news. The word *noble* is not used sarcastically here. The practice of journalism has, in most democracies, special protections and rights because it is one of the people's defences against tyranny and injustice. Tabloid stories—let's call them hot-stuff stories—are not likely to inspire the people to rise against their oppressors. (Although many believe that hot-stuff TV dramas like *Dallas,* seen in East Germany, helped bring down the Wall.)

So hot stuff is not part of the core competencies of journalism: politics and business. It has no advice for us on our democratic responsibilities and duties. It may tell us something of the character of powerful people; but it is silent on the systems and processes that rule us. It neither deep-backgrounds nor spins.

Nor is hot stuff related to another accepted use of journalism: to determine whether or not we are safe. Stories about war, crime, disasters and the environment are all said to answer the important questions: Is my family safe? Is my community safe? Is my world safe? But few of us can learn much that we did not know about safety from Princess Diana's death. We had already decided whether or not to do up our seat belts and ask our chauffeurs to slow down in Paris tunnels.

Hot stuff is not "news you can use," as are stories about health, consumerism, hobbies and education. And I would argue that it is not truly human interest, as are features about feisty centenarians and champion pumpkin carvers. The characters in hot stuff are truly characters: the demonic killers, the fabulous babes, the hot commander in chief and the angelic princess. They are dramatis personae.

Hot stuff certainly fills one of the chief purposes of journalism, which is to sell copies and increase ratings. This has always been important, but it is especially so today as publicly traded news businesses battle for shareholder value. The *Columbia Journalism Review,* in an entire issue devoted to what it calls "money lust," opines that "more so than at any other moment in journalism's history—the news product that lands on newsstands, doorsteps, and television screens is hurt by a heightened, unseemly lust at many companies for ever greater profits." The periodical warns that today's "diminished and deracinated journalism . . . could lead to a fatal erosion of the ancient bond between journalists and the public."

Both Walter Cronkite and Brenda Starr agree. A saddened Brenda, holding a wineglass firmly, gives her view: "Sometimes I think newspapers care more about profits than they do about people." And Walter Cronkite says that today's television corporate leaders show little understanding of their responsibilities to the public. News executives know better, he says, but they are "helpless when top management demands an increase in ratings to protect profits."

Certainly if profits are the question, hot stuff is one terrific answer. In the past five years, hot stuff has produced all of the utterly ecstatic revenue moments of the news business. From the first shot of the white Bronco on the freeway, O. J. drove CNN ratings, revenue and stock prices. *Time* and *Newsweek*'s covers on Diana—two each in a row—produced the biggest newsstand sales in the magazines' histories. CBC Newsworld drew huge audiences even at midnight the night Diana died. The numbers for her funeral service were as much as 60 times higher than normal.

The Diana phenomenon was the breathtaking culmination of a change in news choices that had begun years before. The *Times* in London probably shows that change most dramatically. As an occasional reader since the 1960s, I haven't had the opportunity of regular readers to be immunized against its new forces. I get wheezy and disconcerted when I read a *Times* front page devoted to Kate Moss, David Beckham and Alexander (no relation) McQueen. Turning to the court circular helps restore my normal heart rate. The *Economist* has noted that in a newspaper historically celebrated for its international news (Stanley finds Livingstone, the Charge of the Light Brigade), the *Times'* front page recently had only one foreign piece: it was about Leonardo DiCaprio's new girlfriend.

Rupert Murdoch had a heretical vision. Like many other heretical visions, it has become commonplace. The Project for Excellence in Journalism analyzed stories on television, newsmagazines and front pages and concluded that stories of celebrity, gossip and scandal took up 43 percent of the total space—three time more than 20 years ago. It all seems to have worked out nicely. Profits at most newspaper chains are showing healthy gains, and television news departments have become profit centres.

Although one critic dismisses "giving the people what they want" as a drug pusher's argument, the fact is that none of these choices and changes would have been made if the public had not responded. Hot stuff sells; people watch it and buy it in huge numbers. Even well-educated, responsible and decent people like you and me get hooked. Right now I'm reading every word of the *Globe and Mail*'s comprehensive and straight-faced coverage of the trial of a Richmond Hill, Ontario, dominatrix. (I'm puzzled why one of the policemen who raided her establishment chose to lick the high-heeled boots of a staff member. Perhaps later testimony will enlighten me.)

It is important to consider also that hot-stuff journalism brings the storyteller and the audience directly together.

Journalists who are concerned about the increasing dominance (do not see above) of scandal and gossip in news might do well to consider why it is so popular. There are many theories.

Margaret Thatcher had one of them when she said that "there is no such thing as society: only individuals and their families." In her time, politicians, associations and even nation states began to be seen as ineffective and even irrelevant (incorrectly seen so, in my view). Philosopher Mark Kingwell in his book *Better Living* says this is an age in which "the individual is granted an unprecedented moral, political and epistemological influence." So it is hardly surprising that the intensely personal—indeed the intimate—becomes an important subject of journalism.

Another, simpler theory is that ordinary people are rather stupid, moving their lips as they read the latest about Brad Pitt, content to take their daily dose of soma, uninterested in anything but sensation and titillation. Although there is a definite bozo factor in the population, it is my experience that most people want to expand their experience. People are eager to learn, eager to be involved in the world and, most of all, intensely curious. Working at the Discovery Channel, where a hot-stuff story is the uncovering of a new dinosaur skeleton, I'm constantly humbled by the knowledge and the intelligence of our general public.

But Discovery Channel's ratings hit their lowest the week of August 31, 1997 —the week of Diana's death. Our viewers had the same fascination for the Diana story as everyone else's.

And it was a Story. That is an important reason, I believe, for the attraction of hot stuff. Hot-stuff journalism may seem trivial and irrelevant. But most of it has the pure and elemental force of the story. There is a narrative; there are characters. Storytelling is simply the most powerful form of human communication. We are wired to absorb and comprehend the world through constructing, telling and hearing stories—our own and others'.

But journalism is more than storytelling. It is about getting at the truth. It is about witnessing faithfully and intelligently, it is about recording carefully, it is about hard questioning and intense listening, and it is about skepticism and empathy. But when all of that is done, there is still a story to tell. And in most traditional journalism, from daily news to documentaries, this is the element most forgotten. There are dangers to journalistic storytelling: sometimes the facts don't fit a neat narrative; bits have to be crammed in or left out. But much as we may wish it were not so, the story rules. It will always be irresistible to humans. And the essence of hot stuff is a simple, dramatic story. Unless journalists are willing to study the craft of storytelling so they can apply it to subjects that are difficult and foreign but relevant, they will fight a losing battle against the natural story. And why should the Devil have all the good tunes?

It is important to consider also that hot-stuff journalism brings the storyteller and audience directly together. Political, business or labour reporters all want and need the respect of those about whom they write. These journalists may be willing to irritate or even anger their subjects, but they want to be seen as knowledgeable and clever about the issues. The result is often a kind of insider writing that puts the onus on the viewer or reader to fight his or her way into the inner sanctum where the reporter and subject live. In much of hot-stuff reporting, that's not so. No journalist really cared what Monica Lewinsky or Louise Woodward thought about their press. The reporters were free to think only about the viewers and their needs. The result is often clearer, more vivid writing; inviting to everyone, excluding no one.

However, hot stuff has another appeal: the moral questions it raises. When I was a young journalist, idealistic, arrogant and hopeful, I thought my profession might change the world—expose injustice, inspire citizenship, provoke thought, preserve democracy, increase decency. Although I am still hopeful, I am more realistic now about my former profession and about the world. One of my early exposures to realism came when a friend told me that he used CBC-TV's *The National* as a sort of countrywide weather report. A journalist reporting in front of daffodils at the Victoria legislature told my friend that spring had arrived there; parka-clad Halifax strikers filling the air with frosty-breathed slogans informed him of cold weather in the Maritimes. All the information we had carefully gathered, shaped and presented was casually dismissed by my friend, who used our work for his own personal purposes. We were not in control.

Later I read a survey of people who described the uses they made of journalism. They found news to be very important in their lives; but they did not say they used it to help them fulfill the duties of citizenship or to decide their economic courses of action or to galvanize themselves into political action. They used the news as something to talk about. How trivial, I thought, raging. They see the world as small talk. Again, we were not in control.

Perhaps when we gather in the lunchroom to discuss O.J. or Paul Bernardo or Paula Jones or Alan Eagleson or Princess Diana, we are really discussing our moral options and ourselves.

I now think that using the news as something to talk about is terribly important. I think it may even be the way of linking information to personal decisions: what American cultural critic Neil Postman might call adding wisdom to data.

And I suspect that one of the appeals of hot-stuff journalism is that it gives people a simple and effective opportunity to explore and discuss morals and ethics; to test their own standards and principles; to answer Socrates' question "What is the life that is worth living?"

In our daily lives, we make many more ethical decisions than we do political ones. We will be called on to vote perhaps once a year. But every day we face moral decisions. There are small ones: Should I give money to a squeegee kid? Should I walk back four blocks to return the extra $10 the cashier gave me? Is that man lying on the street drunk or sick? What should I do about him? And there are horrific dilemmas: my unborn child is deformed; my dying father begs me to help him go sooner. Or how do we deal with a nasty neighbour, a daughter-in-law of a very different religion, a drug-addicted friend? What does it mean to be a good parent, spouse, child or employee? Perhaps when we gather in the lunchroom to discuss O.J. or Paul Bernardo or Paula Jones or Alan Eagleson or Princess Diana, we are really discussing our moral options and ourselves.

There is a paradox here: people clearly seek out and desire information about morality; and they are just as clearly rejecting more of the traditional sources of that information.

Organized religions, the former holders of the great code, are attractive to fewer and fewer Canadians. Although 83 percent of Canadians still say they believe in God, only about 30 percent go to services regularly. Pollster Michael Adams, in his book *Sex in the Snow,* writes that Canadians are giving up on traditional religious dogma in favour of a less guilt-ridden spirituality, and in the process are rejecting most traditional authority. "After killing God," he writes, "we 'killed' all the 'fathers' in our lives, whether they sat across from us at the dinner table, stood at the front of our classrooms, signed our pay cheques, or determined our laws."

The Pollara research firm (motto: we know what you're thinking) publishes a yearly Public Trust Index. In 1998 it showed an across-the-board shift toward a lower degree of trust concerning almost all professions. Even the most highly trusted professionals—nurses, pharmacists and doctors—scored lower and registered higher levels of distrust.

With all the traditional sources of ethical inspiration in disrepute, we are starting to see results. Younger people, those born during what Michael Adams calls above "the killing of the fathers," seem to be more dishonest—and not afraid to tell pollsters that's the way it is. Anton L. Allahar, co-author of *Generation on Hold: Coming of Age in the Late Twentieth Century,* says of young people: "They are hedonistic, individualistic and materialistic. They have no concern for civic duty. We live in a dog-eat-dog society."

Both the Insurance Bureau of Canada and Allan Gregg's Strategic Counsel say that people between 18 and 29 have a weaker attachment to ethical standards. Gregg puts a comforting analysis on this, noting the group's full tolerance of diversity in lifestyles, and posits that the "rejection of a strong moral code can be interpreted not as a lack of ethical standards, but as a desire to allow others to pursue their lives and goals, unencumbered by restrictive notions. If they have a credo, it might be 'Do your own thing.'" Or: 'There is no such thing as society.'"

And yet, in the Strategic Counsel poll, while 96 percent thought the two key values in life were individual ones—having a fulfilling job and being in a good relationship—82 percent still ranked living to a high moral standard as important. That's well below the 93 percent who thought physical fitness was a key value, but strong evidence that Socrates was plugged in. We know where to go to get physically fit, but the Gold's Gym of ethics isn't available yet.

To replace the now-distrusted traditional sources of ethical inspiration, North Americans are increasingly turning to self-help books. The yogic prescriptions of Dr. Deepak Chopra are bestsellers, as are the inspirational *Chicken Soup for the Soul* books. *Don't Sweat the Small Stuff,* a book that prescribes moral exercises (begin each day with a loving thought) to relieve stress, has been on the bestseller lists for more than a year.

But in spite of the demand for, and the scarcity of, credible sources of information on ethics, mainstream journalism is curiously absent from this arena. It offers "news you can use" on almost every subject: RRSPs, removing stains, starting a neighbourhood action group, writing a résumé, taking vitamins. It educates us endlessly on politics, personal finance and health. But on ethics and spirituality, the great presses and the great networks can offer only whispers. There are a few religion columns and essays. Business ethics receive some attention, and journalistic ethics are covered. CBC Newsworld, in fact, has announced a program for the fall season entitled *The Moral Divide.* It is probably the first of its kind. Perhaps it is the first of a trend.

It makes me squeamish to try to "sell" journalism about ethics, but I think it is possible to find utility as well as virtue in the subject. It may even be useful to achieve what seems to be the three goals of the premillennium period: happiness, autonomy and materialism.

Mark Kingwell's search for the nature of happiness in *Better Living* brought him to this conclusion: "The only possible way the notion of happiness can be reclaimed from the machinery of manipulation and self-indulgence is to recast it as the possession of virtuous character and the performance of virtuous action. I want to agree with Russell's insight . . . that the happy life is to an extraordinary extent the same as the good life." And Kingwell also sees the achievement of the virtuous life as true autonomy: "I know that my feelings and judgements of happiness are safely mine as long as I have the strength of mind to make them so."

And, finally, there are the uses of ethics in the material world. In his book *Trust,* Francis Fukuyama argues that national economies rely not only on physical and human capital, but on social capital: the degree of trust that members of society have for one another. He agrees with Max Weber that capitalism came into being not because of economic conditions, but because of cultural ones. A certain set of virtues—frugality, truth-telling, a sense of justice, respect for law, and disciplined hard work—provided the habits of mind that encouraged entrepreneurship. Fukuyama believes that trust—the belief that others will act honestly—is an economic asset. When trust erodes, as he sees happening in North America, the economy must bear the costs of prisons, lawyers, security guards, bribes and red tape.

The more we consider the importance—the value and the wonderful stories of moral and ethical decisions—the more curious the lack of their presence in journalism is. The Greeks had a word for those unacquainted with ethics: *idiot.*

CONRAD M. BLACK

Conrad M. Black is chairman and chief executive officer of Argus Corporation Limited, Hollinger Inc. and Southam Inc. in Canada; chairman and chief executive officer of Hollinger International Inc. in the United States; and chairman of Telegraph Group Limited in London, England.

Hollinger International Inc. is a multinational company with significant interests in the publishing, printing and distribution of newspapers and magazines in Canada, the United Kingdom, the United States and Israel. It and its affiliates control more than 500 publications with a total circulation of more than 13 million, including 175 daily newspapers with a circulation of 4.5million.

Black holds a bachelor of arts degree from Carleton University, a law degree from Laval University, and master of art degrees from McGill University, the University of Windsor and Carleton University. His autobiography, *A Life in Progress,* made the Canadian bestseller lists in 1993. His earlier book, *Duplessis,* is an authoritative study of modern Quebec history.

The Proliferation of Choice Guarantees Stronger Newspapers

I KNOW OF FEW TOPICS that are so regularly the subject of cant and charlatanism as the future of the media. The obsequies of the newspaper business have been pronounced so often, and by so many, that it should now resemble the silent-movie or black-and-white television industries. In fact, the newspaper business is as prosperous as ever, and in this country, possibly more profitable than it has ever been.

Of course, newspapers will have to adapt, but reading has not gone altogether out of fashion. Even Bill Gates says that if something is more than two pages long he wants to read it on paper and not on a screen. Screens will never be as portable, as disposable, as easy to read selectively from, as newspapers. Research on a screen is very useful, but reading casually what is scrolled across a screen for more than a few minutes is unspeakably irritating. Have any of those who have been most vocal in tolling the death knell of the printed word ever tried to read lengthily off a screen? I suspect not.

I accept that those newspapers that are read more for entertainment than for information, including most tabloid newspapers, are comparatively vulnerable to electronic competition. Entertainment is more easily provided and received electronically than on newsprint. But newspapers, including virtually all those controlled by Hollinger International Inc., which are read for information, possess franchises based on custom and loyalty to individual writers, perspectives and formats. If the franchise is strong and the content is good, the means of delivery is secondary.

The Internet and other recent electronic innovations have geometrically increased choice. Choice overwhelms and there is no evidence that search engines will ever narrow the gap between the bewildered consumer and the ever-burgeoning variety of matters on offer. The editorial function becomes steadily more important even than it has been. The serendipitous quality of a well-edited newspaper, with an intelligent selection of news, features, sports, business and comment, becomes more important than ever, as the media consumer contemplates the alternatives of swimming upstream against a cascading torrent of undifferentiated transmissions.

If the franchise and the content are strong, the means of delivery can be the option of the subscriber. Some readers will always want newsprint editions. Some will want newspapers from their screens. Some will want designer editions, with individually preselected categories of news and comment highlighted, either on screens or in faxes. Whatever the public wants in commercially sufficient numbers, since the public is always right, we as an industry will provide. As I have said many times before, if readers want our contents towed around the skies of our cities behind blimps, we'll provide that, too.

As choice proliferates, the newspaper industry's position actually strengthens in comparative terms. The endless fragmentation of market among television channels provided by cable and satellite, followed by the vertiginous increase in Internet options, leaves the newspaper without unlimited growth potential in circulation, but with a larger comparative market share than ever. The cake is divided into more and more pieces, but the newspaper's share shrinks less than those directly cannibalized by electronic competition and becomes comparatively larger. Despite considerable erosion, many newspapers are market leaders. The *Windsor Star,* for example, is still read by 81 percent of its market-area adults each week.

In too many cities, including most of those Hollinger entered with its takeover of Southam, the local newspaper has been afflicted with an infelicitous combination of monopolistic arrogance and defeatism in the presence of other media.

I don't wish to sound a premature note of skepticism about our electronic rivals, but the on-line business is not, in commercial terms, a real business.

Hollinger is one of the largest Internet publishers in the world, with more than 70 Web sites, and we have millions of so-called hits every day and well over 100,000 of our pages are read every day from these sites. However, virtually all attempts to charge for on-line access have been unsuccessful, and publishers who are not extremely vigilant can easily spend millions providing their own newspaper free on a screen, undercutting their own paid sale. Many have done so, but Hollinger is not among them.

The newspaper industry must adapt, and I don't mean only with respect to its means of delivery. In many places, content must be improved, as well. In Canada and the United States, the newspaper industry has paid a high price for having so few competitive newspaper cities. The tendency in both countries has been for under-edited, wordy, ashen newspapers that are inaccessible, lack variety and panache, and blur the line between editorial and information thoroughly. In too many cities, including most of those Hollinger entered with its takeover of Southam, the local newspaper has been afflicted with an infelicitous combination of monopolistic arrogance and defeatism in the presence of other media. Here, too, the newspaper must adapt and recognize that flabby reliance on monopolistic security will lead to other media eating it alive, starting with classified ads, but that resistance is both possible and necessary.

By purchasing largely mismanaged newspapers at bargain prices, Hollinger has built up its newspaper business in the past 11 years from a very modest 40,000 daily circulation—mainly in the smaller centres of British Columbia—to a daily circulation of 4.7 million and a prodigious nondaily circulation. Many publishers, like generals trying to refight World War II, have been unprepared and unable to adjust to the spectre of the electronic invasion, so we took advantage of the situation.

Almost invariably the cost structure can be shaken down as the product is improved by better editing which, of course, requires more effort by many journalists. As the newspaper industry became more perplexed or demoralized, excessive collegiality and unionistic rigidity were often added to the overmanning that frequently arose in the industry's easy years. I have yet to encounter a fundamentally viable newspaper that didn't respond to the elimination of superfluous personnel, the reformation of the culture of the workplace, an injection of editorial panache and variety, and the assertion of that newspaper's commercial and professional right to life.

In commerce, Grade 3 arithmetic is ultimately unanswerable. As personnel, and for a time, raw material costs have come down, revenues have been raised by reanimated sales forces, causing newspapers to revive financially, as well as morally, whenever management possesses leadership capacity. As products have been made more lively and alluring, the long-standing decline in circulation has been generally arrested, and in many places, including at the *Calgary Herald,* reversed.

In all of these emerging circumstances, I believe the convergence that will be achieved will be that of the screen. All television—paid, satellite and terrestrial—and the Internet will be on the same screen. Logging on will be almost instantaneous and, as a practical matter, everything will be available on the same screen.

Richard Perle, the chairman of Hollinger Digital, our electronic and advanced technology business, tells me his neighbourhood doughnut shop is on the Internet. In this new world of infinite choice and unlimited access, newspapers will put their own news and game shows, movie and sports, arts and specialty channels on the Internet and cross-promote these channels with the newspaper itself in all its printed, faxed and televised manifestations. This process must start with classified advertising, where most serious newspaper publishers have already moved to protect themselves with combination newspaper and on-line classified sales. Failure to protect classified advertising in this way will result in the loss of the entire classified business.

As we approach the version of convergence I have described, it is not the newspaper that will be endangered but the insouciant, isolated or overpaying licence holder. Why buy a television licence when in fewer than 10 years, picture clarity, swiftness of response and availability will be practically identical between licensed channels and Richard Perle's doughnut shop? The newspapers, cross-supporting with their own Internet channels and thus achieving a huge marketing advantage, will pool overheads, avoid licensing costs and have only programming expenditures to contend with. I don't see this as spending my declining years in the buggy-whip business. I see before me, in more than one sense, my proverbial golden years.

I suppose I should say a word about the rather hackneyed question of media ownership. I accept that the fact that Hollinger owns a little more than 40 percent of the daily newspaper circulation of Canada is, on its face, a fact that justifies legitimate public interest. And, of course, because of the media's potential for influencing public opinion, it is a question the public and national interest should monitor carefully.

However, in a time when millions of homes take much of their information off the Internet, most homes receive scores of television channels, and almost all Canadian cities have home delivery of more than one newspaper, traditional criteria of measuring media competition are very outmoded. Instead of agitating and litigating over percentages of Canadian newspapers or newspaper circulation, I suggest we take up the formula that has been recently discussed, though not yet adopted, in Britain and Australia. We should devise a system of estimating media units of circulation for all types of media, establishing a basis of equivalence for listening, viewing and reading statistics and imposing a limit of ownership, say, 20 or 25 percent of all media, that any single corporation can own. The notion that was audible in Canada early in 1997 that owning 40 percent of the paid daily newspaper circulation of this country constitutes an ability to manipulate public opinion or constrict freedom of expression is almost unimaginably absurd. The country's public policy debate didn't miss much when the judiciary declined in December 1996 to hear this argument.

It is clear from the history of the newspaper industry that using newspapers for systematic propaganda or vendettas leads directly to the evaporation of the franchise. Hollinger saw that in London with the *Observer* when it was owned by Lonrho. It was a flying carpet for its proprietor's capricious likes and hates and lost 40 percent of its circulation in 10 years to the *Sunday Times* and *Sunday Telegraph*.

It is complicating enough in our commercial lives to be accused of being a corporate dinosaur wallowing in a dying business without being reviled at the same time as a propaganda monopoly. According to this theory, Hollinger is plotting to transform the Canadian public into a witless lumpen bourgeoisie chanting obedience to a range of extreme causes that my associates and I do not, in fact, support. I trust the public debate has not descended to the unfathomable depths where I am expected to respond further to the pathological inanities of Maude Barlow and Clayton Ruby. We will give Canada a more professionally distinguished daily press regardless of what Barlow and her ragged army of performing feminist-socialist robots thinks of it.

I trust the public debate has not descended to the unfathomable depths where I am expected to respond further to the pathological inanities of Maude Barlow and Clayton Ruby.

One of the most important elements of this pledge is simply to write better, to use the language more imaginatively, more graphically, more literately; to write lighter, more rigorous, less opinionated stories. People will respond to good writing. I don't mean laborious, excessive detail, pedantry, stridency or the sophomoric journalistic fad in North America of journalists who think they are investigative Bob Woodwards and stylistic Ernest Hemingways. In the vortex of defeatism and overconfidence I described earlier, such sloppy habits took root in most Canadian and American newspapers.

The problem was aggravated by the separation between the responsibility for corporate results and for product content. In none of the other industries represented here would chief executives have consented to be praised for having absolutely nothing to do with the quality, nature or content of the product. Nor should the publishers and corresponding executives in other media be lightly excused for allowing the Left in the working press successfully to represent proprietary vigilance for professional standards as abusive interference with editorial integrity. This insane segregation of commercial and editorial management was elevated into a cardinal virtue as editors and journalists praised noninterventionist newspaper executives while they highjacked their products and became either bland or antagonistic to the communities being served. This was like the head of Coca-Cola saying he didn't care how his beverages tasted, or the head of General Motors saying he didn't care what his cars looked like or whether they actually worked.

The *Calgary Herald* was a case in point. Here was a newspaper that was antagonistic to the overwhelmingly popular provincial government, hostile to the petroleum industry, and represented virtually no one within 500 miles of Calgary. Declining circulation wasn't the result of a malaise in the newspaper industry; it was the result of a system incapable of producing a product that would attract those it was intended to serve.

That system has been dismembered and the *Herald*'s circulation is rising. I don't believe that Canadians, whose country is the most wire-cabled in the world, who have virtually all the media of the United States as well as of Canada on their menu, are threatened by lack of diversity. To the extent that they are, it is by conformity of opinion among the so-called working press, not by cartelism among the proprietors.

To reiterate, the greatest problems in the newspaper industry of this country are not concentration of ownership but slipshod professional standards and defeatism about the viability of the industry. Most journalists, like most people, are honest and competent men and women trying to do their jobs conscientiously. But, as in other organizations and other types of work, when professional standards are not imposed, they will not be as well maintained by self-regulation. This is no disrespect to journalists. When management, in this case editorial management, doesn't manage, the employees manage for themselves with mixed results. In the case of the newspaper industry in North America in the 1970s and 1980s, there was too much sanctimonious talk about the sacred trust of the journalist and too many slovenly work practices—not enough objective reporting and too much self-serving advocacy.

I don't believe these problems would have become as serious as they did without the propagation of the rather exaggerated theory that American republican institutions and the U.S. Constitution were saved by a couple of investigative journalists supported by Ben Bradlee and Katharine Graham in the Watergate affair. Nor could these problems have been as prolonged without the economic and technological challenges that beset the newspaper industry in the past 10 years and incapacitated the management of many companies. But these problems do respond to a modicum of leadership and a genuine appeal to the professional integrity of the working press.

A product less irritating to the average fair-minded reader, apart from being a higher expression of the journalistic craft, strengthens the franchise and enhances the job security of the working press. It is not, in all but the most severely afflicted newspapers, a particularly hard transition to make.

I suppose something should be said about the issue of privacy and journalistic ethics. I yield to few in my dislike of the antics of sensational media and of insensitive journalists, but neither had much to do with the tragic death of Princess Diana. The cause of her fatal accident was excessive speed compounded by not using seat belts. The driver, whatever his level of sobriety, would not have been going 120 miles per hour in a 30-mile-per-hour zone if the back-seat passengers had told him to be more careful. Both the princess and Dodi Fayed frequently used the tabloid press for their own ends, and the last trip wouldn't have been known about at all if the Fayeds hadn't advised the *Daily Mail*'s chief gossip columnist they were travelling to Italy and Paris together. Nor was the Ritz Hotel on Saturday night the most imaginative venue if Dodi and Diana were seeking to be inconspicuous.

It pains me to come to the defence of the least attractive form of journalism, but they are substantially innocent of this terrible accident, and Earl Spencer's remarks on the subject, and on some other topics, at Diana's funeral, though eloquent and heartfelt, were, to say the least, ill-considered.

Hollinger's position, as an owner of newspapers that have always had a policy of not publishing inappropriately obtained or salacious photographs, is that attempts to legislate content or taste other than for defamation or gross indecency are impossible without affronting the concept of a free press. But we are in favour of civil, or in extreme cases, criminal liability for publication of illegally obtained material. Photographs taken on a public street are not in this category, but zoom photographs such as those taken of the Duchess of York a few years ago by an enterprising French photographer are another matter, particularly since the man trespassed and crawled on his stomach like a snake for a mile to shoot the pictures.

With that said, some of the affected pieties of tabloid publishers and editors in London in the aftermath of Diana's death were outrageous. To have David English, chairman of Associated Newspapers, as head of the Code Committee of the Press Complaints Commission is like appointing Al Capone to head a commission to investigate organized crime in Chicago in the 1920s. At one point, the *Daily Mail* ran a headline that said "Charles Weeps Bitter Tears of Guilt," which was a monstrous intrusion and a complete fabrication. In our own *Daily Telegraph*, we ran an editorial that same week that made it clear that this form of pervasive hypocrisy and mendacity, this philosophy of intrusion, couldn't really be legislated against, but it was still evil.

So, apart from minor legislative fine-tuning, there is little to be done other than for certain public figures to be more judicious and discreet, certain media bosses to be less hypocritical and dishonest, and people generally to be more discerning so that they reward good behaviour in public figures and professional integrity in the media and punish their absence.

This essay was adapted from remarks made by Conrad Black in September 1997 at the Spruce Meadows international round table, an event organized annually by Calgary businessman Ron Southern.

VINCENT CARLIN

Vincent Carlin is chair of the Ryerson School of Journalism. He was the head of CBC Newsworld, and brings to Ryerson a distinguished background in print and broadcast journalism. His previous management experience includes positions as senior director for information programs and chief news editor, CBC Television; and managing editor of CBC Radio News.

A graduate of Georgetown University and former visiting fellow at the Institute for Policy Studies at Duke University, Carlin served as a correspondent in Washington for *Time* and was subsequently bureau chief for Time-Life News Service in Montreal.

His television experience consists of stints as producer of the Montreal supper-hour program, *City at Six;* chief of CBC's parliamentary bureau; host of the Newsworld program *Media;* and senior producer of the Gemini Award–winning series, *Witness.* In radio he has been chief correspondent for CBC Radio News; anchor and writer of *World Report;* and host of *Media File.*

The Good, the Bad and the Ugly of Corporate Newspaper Control

THE LANDSCAPE OF BUSINESS TODAY reminds me of those representations of how the land was formed here on Earth. Masses of molten material collided and recoiled, then recombined and congealed. Some of what resulted turned into lush grasslands and forests, fruitful and productive for everyone. But there were also deserts and mountains that were of use only to specially adapted creatures.

Everywhere we look today businesses are recombining and concentrating. All use the same mantra: Bigness is not bad. It's necessary. It's the only way to compete in today's global economy. Banks, funeral homes, department stores all talk the same talk.

Other sectors go one better. Using the mantra of "synergy," businesses pyramid the cash from one business into leverage over others. Seagram, for example, is using its liquor profits to build a huge entertainment complex: movie and television studios, record companies. Some foresee the day when Seagram forsakes the liquor business entirely.

The argument for this kind of acquisitiveness almost always contains that word *synergy*. My *American Heritage Dictionary of the English Language* defines synergy as "the interaction of two or more agents or forces so that their combined effect is greater than the sum or their individual effects," or the corporate world "cooperative interaction among groups, especially among the acquired subsidiaries or merged parts of a corporation, that creates an enhanced combined effect."

In plain language that would be one corporate partner washing the paws of another. We saw this most recently, and disastrously, when the CNN and *Time* branches of Time-Warner "synergized" their way into an embarrassing foul-up over a story about the alleged use of poison gas during the Vietnam War. In that case the "enhanced combined effect" was almost totally negative.

It was the potential of that kind of conglomerate ownership that so troubled the Royal Commission on Newspapers (popularly called the Kent Commission) in 1981. The commission was set up in the wake of what appeared to be a "deal" to limit competition between supposedly competing newspaper chains. Its view of the landscape, as outlined in its report, was bleak: "Newspaper competition, of the kind that used to be, is virtually dead in Canada. The only market where there is anything like the old head-on competition, between two papers published at the same time of day and competing across the community is French-speaking Montreal." The commissioners went on to say that "The concentration of ownership in chains is, in the commission's view, bad. It should not have been permitted."

At the time, it appeared that Canadian newspapers would eventually fall under the control of companies that made most of their money outside the newspaper business. Since there was decreasing competition, the commission was understandably concerned.

For many journalists and academics of a certain age, there is a pleasing nostalgia attached to the days of intense competition in the big cities and family-owned local papers in the smaller communities. In fact, the "competition" was often over insignificant but flashy events, much like the competition today among "tabloid" television shows. And not every small-city publisher was a benevolent soul with only the good of the community at heart. Just like today's barons, these publishers were businessmen who paid close attention to profits. They were closer to their readers, but equally close to their advertisers. (Today, of course, owners are more likely found with advertisers than readers.)

The Kent Commission's report is tinged with that sense of nostalgia, of a time past when issues of public policy came before notions of profit, when publishers acted in the public interest, not for private gain. While the commissioners' rearview mirror might have been foggy, their crystal ball also appears to have been clouded. When they wrote their report, Conrad Black had only a minor newspaper presence largely through small-market papers concentrated in British Columbia, the *Toronto Sun* was just beginning to make healthy profits, widespread use of the Internet did not exist, and all newspapers were printed on bulky and expensive presses. The personal computer had been invented but hadn't reached desktops yet, and "surfing" was something done by characters in songs by the Beach Boys.

So, just as the world has changed dramatically in the past quarter century, our view of what is good and bad about ownership patterns must also undergo a reality test. We might all agree that it would be preferable if newspapers were locally owned and run as public trusts, but we might also all agree it would be preferable if all Canadians were bilingual. Both are laudable ideals; both are unachievable in the real world. Therefore, we will have to deal with reality and, as a starting point, who better to begin with than Conrad Black?

Black's Hollinger Incorporated began life as a holding company with a varied assortment of industrial properties in its portfolio. But Black always seemed ill at ease as a supermarket mogul or the head of a tractor company. His corporate manoeuvring in those fields led to lawsuits and bad publicity. He had made his first noninherited money in the newspaper business with his pal Peter White at the *Sherbrooke Record*, and wanted to continue in that way. However, despite casting his lot with newspapers, he had few Canadian assets because, as he once said, "There don't seem to be any available." But that would soon change.

At this point in his journey, Black had not yet acquired control of Southam, the jewel in his Canadian crown. But while other companies were retrenching or selling to conglomerates, Black was more interested in buying and expanding. And, truth be told, he clearly radiated a sense of enjoyment in the role that he publicly disdained: media mogul.

In the "old days," journalists liked their owners rich and dim or, at least, uninvolved.

Today Black has expanded his reach on the international level (London's *Daily Telegraph*, the *Jerusalem Post*, the *Chicago Sun-Times*) and, in fact, has become someone many journalists and academics love to hate. He controls a majority of the daily newspaper titles in Canada and some 40 percent of the circulation. He makes his views known in a stentorian, multisyllabic style and operates with considerable panache on an international stage.

In the "old days," journalists liked their owners rich and dim or, at least, uninvolved. They had to be rich to sustain the paper, but if they were too smart, or too involved, one might have had to answer to them in more detail than a blanket assertion of the sanctity of freedom of the press.

In more recent years, owners have become more remote and corporate. The Kent Commission had taken as its theme the threat to competition posed by conglomerate ownership. In fact, the commission conceded the reality of monopoly ownership in many cities and suggested ways to stimulate the growth of newspaper companies, but they were not to grow too big: "Under existing law and policy, the process of concentration will continue to a bitterer end: company will take over company, agglomeration will proceed, until all Canadian newspapers are divisions of one or two great conglomerates."

Well, neither law nor policy changed, but the conglomerates decided that the newspaper business was not to their liking. At the time of the Kent

Commission report, the *Toronto Sun* was still a fledgling paper, just beginning to make a healthy profit. As the self-styled Little Newspaper That Grew, the *Sun* revelled in its image as the people's paper—as the smart-ass tabloid that stood for common sense amid the pompous platitudes of its competition. It was born out of the wreckage of the *Toronto Telegram,* a much mythologized daily that was shut down by John Bassett, its millionaire owner, when it looked as if unions might get what he thought was too much money for their workers. However, in the obituaries for the paper, and the more recent obituaries for Bassett himself, attention was often focused on stunts and bizarre individuals rather than on the highest standards of Canadian journalism.

The *Toronto Sun,* however, was largely owned by the people who were running it. Disagreements among them were charmingly played out in the pages of the paper. If Conrad Black wanted his big papers to emulate London's *Daily Telegraph* in literacy and intellectual pretension, the *Sun*'s owners wanted their paper to be relentlessly simple in language and plebeian in outlook. If so-called mainstream journalists love to dislike Conrad Black, they also love to disparage the *Toronto Sun:* dumb, working-class, opinionated and, well, tabloid.

They also share a general right-of-centre view of the world, with Sun Media in the populist camp and Hollinger somewhat more establishment intellectual.

For those of us who grew up with tabloids, it was clear that the *Sun* was an interesting and well-produced variant. It certainly wasn't dumb; it just didn't take itself as seriously as the broadsheets. Plebeian it might be, but those who work there would probably take that as a compliment, if it meant they were identifying with the common person. Opinionated, certainly. Its news stories were brash, although rarely inaccurate. Its columns were generally to the right of centre, but with populist overtones and enough internal disagreement to make it interesting. Tabloid: well, yes, that was the point.

And the *Toronto Sun* did grow and grow. *Suns* rose across the country, and the chain, Sun Media Corporation, acquired smaller newspaper and magazine titles. It endured a period of corporate ownership when it was taken over by Maclean Hunter, but when, in the North American pattern, Maclean Hunter was acquired by yet another company, Rogers Communications, Sun Media was sold off to other investors, including the papers' managers. Leading that group was Paul Godfrey, who had earlier parlayed his Metro Toronto Council chairman job into a powerful position as publisher of the *Toronto Sun*.

Now Sun Media, with Godfrey as CEO, has assumed a position as the second-largest newspaper chain in Canada. It has broadened its base from one Toronto tabloid to other big city tabs to the medium-size city broadsheet and the small-town daily and weekly. It also has a stake in the new media: the Web-based CANOE service and the cable-based Toronto TV news operation, CablePulse 24. But the bedrock is the newspaper business. Its corporate strategy appears to be based on a combination of unique vehicles (the *Suns* in Ottawa, Calgary, Edmonton and, of course, Toronto) and monopoly markets (*London Free Press* and its new acquisitions from Southam in Hamilton, Kitchener-Waterloo, Cambridge and Guelph).

Meanwhile, the Thomson Corporation, whose newspaper chain used to dominate Canada's small and midsize markets, is left with a corporal's guard of titles that includes, besides the *Globe and Mail*, the *Winnipeg Free Press*, the *Brandon Sun* and the *Lethbridge Herald*. Clearly Thomson has decided that the Canadian newspaper business is not a major factor in its corporate plans.

The two companies now dominating the national scene share some characteristics and not others. The most obvious similarity is that they are newspaper companies: Hollinger/Southam on the international scene; Sun Media on the domestic. A small inner circle runs both. For Hollinger, Conrad Black and his longtime associates David Radler and Peter White; for Sun Media, Paul Godfrey and a management committee that includes all the heads of the chain's various newspapers. They also share a general right-of-centre view of the world, with Sun Media in the populist camp and Hollinger somewhat more establishment intellectual.

However, the two companies diverge in some interesting ways. Hollinger was built on monopoly markets. That strategy has now been successfully adapted from its small-market roots to the big-city markets in Canada. Sun Media, on the other hand, comes out of the rough-and-tumble tradition of newspaper wars. The *Suns* entered markets in which there was competition, but carved out niches for themselves. They were inadvertently aided in the early days by the smug attitudes of the broadsheet journalists and publishers.

Now, as Sun Media refashions itself as a large and varied newspaper publisher, it appears that it will adapt some of the strategies we have seen pursued by Southam and Hollinger. At the same time, Hollinger has apparently chosen the route of competition in launching a direct challenge to Thomson's *Globe and Mail*. After failing to buy the *Globe*, Conrad Black settled for the *Financial Post*, the other national competitor. Thomson, somewhat uncharacteristically, seems ready to put up a fight, although it remains to be seen how much it will risk in that fight before selling out to either Black or some other interested buyer.

No matter what one thinks of the ideologies of Sun Media or Hollinger, both seem to be trying to raise the quality of their papers while running their businesses more efficiently. The question is whether those two goals are incompatible, and if they are not, whether they can be achieved without the high degree of concentration that is taking place.

Quality in newspapers does not arise spontaneously from below; it has to be encouraged and rewarded from above. Whether at papers owned by individuals like the legendary T. H. Preston of the *Brantford Expositor,* or at chains like Southam's, quality writing and reporting happened because owners demanded it. On the other hand, the Thomson chain is known for emphasizing profit and pays little attention to the actual quality of its journalism. The result is a group of largely mediocre papers, the *Globe and Mail* being a signal exception and not really representative of the chain as a whole.

With close to three-quarters of Canada's newspaper business now dominated by two companies, it is necessary to look at how those companies have worked (and guess how they might work in the future) before we can automatically conclude that concentration is necessarily bad.

The Kent Commission was right about one thing: the days of widespread daily competition in most cities has passed. It had been assumed that a lack of competition would, perforce, lead to lesser quality. In the past decade, that assumption was apparent in many cities. In the English market, only Toronto had a thriving, competitive marketplace with three well-edited, interesting papers at hand. In other cities, particularly London, Winnipeg and Ottawa, once-proud papers were pale in comparison to their predecessors.

Today, though, this situation seems to have changed in several of those places. The *London Free Press,* under Sun Media ownership, has improved noticeably in content and presentation. In Ottawa, Conrad Black's Southam chain dramatically revamped the *Citizen,* improving local coverage as well as adding columns of analysis and comment. As with many Black-inspired publications, the *Citizen* often indulges in the arch and the precious, but those who like good writing can often find comfort there.

Throughout the Hollinger/Southam chain, the look and feel of the larger papers changed, most often for the better. I rush to point out that those improvements are most celebrated by commentators; circulation has not increased appreciably overall, although profits have. Also, some of the improvements appear to have come at the expense of the smaller newspapers in the group. In a letter to the magazine *Next City,* Professor James Winter, a prominent critic of Black's philosophy and style, referred to the way the media mogul runs his business as "vampire journalism," where the blood is sucked out of the papers, particularly the smaller ones.

For its part, Sun Media has not tried to mould its newer acquisitions into a *Sun* format. It also seems to be following a less-combative path with its workers than is often the case with Hollinger's outlets.

It has become part of newspaper folklore that all journalists who are faced with a Hollinger takeover wait for the application of the "Radler formula." In popular mythology, Hollinger associate CEO David Radler counts the number of chairs in a newsroom to figure out how many people can be laid off.

That certainly has been true of the smaller papers that Hollinger has acquired over the years. The only application on a larger scale, however, appears to be the Regina/Saskatoon takeover in 1995 that led to 170 employees of the *Leader-Post* and the *Star-Phoenix* being laid off. Still, it is worth noting that those papers haven't declined in quality and that their former employees have started up new weekly papers in both cities.

Black has steadfastly maintained, with good reason, that he is not a Rupert Murdoch type of newspaper baron who constantly interferes with his papers' policies for the sake of other business interests.

In fact, many of the negative effects predicted for Black-controlled enterprises have not materialized. There is no doubt that Black is an aggressive, opinionated owner. There is also no doubt that many of the properties he has acquired have not declined, and many have improved. We did have to endure a lengthy treatise on international affairs authored by owner Black in the magazine *Saturday Night*, and the highly respected editor Joan Fraser resigned from the *Montreal Gazette* when Black took over, but there has not been the wholesale ideological bloodletting that many predicted.

The Kent Commission felt that real competition could not be reintroduced into many communities because of economic factors, but it feared conglomerate ownership as the potential death of free expression. What has evolved in this country, though, is a newspaper industry that is neither as bad as the commission feared nor as good as it hoped. The industry appears to be healthy in terms of profits, although there is cause for concern about readership. It is not dominated by faceless conglomerates, but rather by highly visible newspaper companies. The range of opinion columns available in most communities is not wide, and certainly the breadth of editorial opinion at the papers themselves tends to be in a fairly narrow range of moderately conservative. Furthermore, that range appears to be narrowing, the *Toronto Star* and some of the Southam papers being notable exceptions.

Conrad Black does not write his papers' editorials. In fact, there is no evidence that he interferes with editorial judgements on a regular basis, but he does hire editors and publishers who share, in a general way, his view of the world. When he disagrees with a paper's stance on a particular issue, he sends it a letter to the editor which, not surprisingly, always gets printed.

Black has steadfastly maintained, with good reason, that he is not a Rupert Murdoch type of newspaper baron who constantly interferes with his papers' policies for the sake of other business interests. A Murdoch-owned publishing company cancelled publication of a book by Chris Patten, the last British governor of Hong Kong. Murdoch said it was not because of the risk of offending his erstwhile business partners in China. He said it was boring. Apologies to Patten ensued.

At the same time Murdoch's newspapers appeared to play down the more negative aspects of developments in China, leading to the not bizarre conclusion that Murdoch did not want to upset the negotiations for a satellite-broadcasting deal with the Chinese.

There is also a particularly Canadian twist to increasing concentration of newspaper ownership. Some of the forces that object most strenuously to the politics of the concentrators (whether Thomson, Sun Media or Hollinger) appear to support measures that enhance the ability of people like Conrad Black to buy up Canadian papers.

Canada has rules that effectively discourage foreign ownership of Canadian newspapers. Therefore, a Canadian with dollars and an interest in the newspaper business has a built-in advantage and little competition. Like many faithful adherents of the free-market system, Conrad Black learned that controlling those markets is good business. His empire was first built on small newspapers that did not face the kind of rigorous competition that dedicated capitalists love to talk about but hate to face. In fact, most were monopoly franchises.

In the current environment, all major publishers are looking for those properties in markets where competition is weak or, preferably, nonexistent. The one exception, of course, is Hollinger's bid to compete directly on the national level. But even there, it turned out to be preferable to swallow at least one competitor—the *Financial Post*—than fight a two-front war.

The fact remains, though, that Canada will end up with another national newspaper, well funded and, if recent experience is any guide, well produced. As much as the anti-Black forces hate to admit it, it appears clear that many of the papers that Hollinger has acquired through Southam are better than they were before.

The environment has changed dramatically since 1981. While our newspapers may retail a narrow range of editorial viewpoints, our television sets and computers allow us to sample widely. We have almost instant access to a range of news and opinion unimaginable a decade ago. Ideas and assertions can be tested immediately, although in a loose and disorganized fashion that would make an academic queasy.

If a decade ago we were worrying about the tight control of a few individuals and corporations on the flow of information, today many observers are troubled about the lack of "gatekeeping" on the World Wide Web. The Matt Drudges and Pierre Bourques have made an art of circulating information that is often unchecked and sometimes uncheckable. Rumours, gossip and outright mischief are retailed widely.

Not so long ago, a man like I. F. Stone was an anomaly: an iconoclastic journalist who stayed at home, pursued topics that interested him and often ended up scooping his well-heeled brethren in the so-called mainstream. While no one from the Web has achieved the stature or respect of Izzy Stone, there are more and more people out there with the means to dig into stories and the ability to "publish" them in many different ways.

The breadth of opinion available on both television and radio is increasingly wide, although too often it runs from moderately conservative to moderately liberal. In the United States, despite the proliferation of cable talk shows, one rarely encounters a truly radical viewpoint.

A viewer can bump into something challenging on Canadian television, particularly on services like CBC Newsworld, and other new cable services also provide forums for the clash of opinions—the kind of conflict that used to be the sole province of newspapers.

More and more, newspapers are playing a different role than they have heretofore. They are still a crucial link in the chain of information, perhaps *the* crucial link, but they are no longer the journals of record of years past. That role is, increasingly, assumed by the Internet. If you want the full text or background on an event, the Internet is the place to find it, as well as a lot of misinformation and trivia, to be sure. And newspaper journalists are no longer the only eyewitnesses to daily events. That role has been taken over by all-news television.

It may be that newspapers in Canada will evolve back toward the European model and become known and read for their particular points of view. Papers such as the *Ottawa Citizen* provide sharp editorial opinions and extra pages of commentary, much like the *Daily Telegraph* in London. It is probable that this style will spread, at least through the Hollinger chain.

The increased concentration of ownership, combined with some of the more outrageous material available on the Internet, have led to calls for regulation, both for the newspaper industry and for the Net. On both counts, the potential cure would be much worse than the disease.

Regulations already in effect helped produce the ownership situation we now face. Further attempts to control ownership, or subsidize new papers, are wrongheaded and would be counterproductive. The only feasible way to stimulate fresh competition for newspaper franchises is to allow new competitors, including non-Canadians, into the field. It might be time to do away with ownership regulations altogether.

Governments rationalized broadcasting regulations because the airwaves were considered to be a scarce public resource. Now that digitized signals and multiplexed channels have dealt with the scarcity question, that rationale is severely weakened. Regulation of any idea-based enterprise, even highly profitable ones like newspapers, is almost always a bad idea. Governments should not be involved in rationing ideas. If "freedom of the press" means anything, it certainly means the freedom to express ideas without government approval.

Of course, in the earlier days of the century, skeptics would say that the only real freedom of the press was for those who owned one. Today almost everyone can run a "press" and find an audience. As smaller-scale entrepreneurs and journalists use the tools at their disposal, as multiple channels make local news coverage easier and more pervasive, and as the big papers face increasing competition from other technologies, we will increasingly have trouble finding the time to digest all the information available to us.

DAVID GALLOWAY

David Galloway was appointed president and chief executive officer of Torstar Corporation in September 1988. Torstar Corporation owns the *Toronto Star,* Canada's largest newspaper; Metroland Publishing and Distributing Ltd., publishers of 35 weekly newspapers; and Harlequin Enterprises Limited. In early 1998, Torstar acquired a 50 percent interest in Sing Tao Newspapers (Canada) Ltd.

Galloway joined Torstar Corporation in 1981. He became president and chief executive officer for Harlequin worldwide in 1982. Prior to joining the Harlequin/Torstar group of companies, for 10 years he was a founding partner of the Canada Consulting Group—a leading strategic management consulting firm, which was acquired by the Boston Consulting Group in 1992. He specialized in the communications industry, including publishing, broadcasting, cable, pay television and film production.

Galloway graduated from Harvard Graduate School of Business with a master in business administration and from the University of Toronto with an honours bachelor of arts in political science and economics.

Why Newspapers Will Flourish in the Years Ahead

IN HOMER'S *Odyssey*, there is a figure named Proteus. He is a sea god who can see into the future. But, more important, he has the ability to change shape to smeet each new challenge. Proteus appears to be an old man. But, when attacked, he can turn into a lion, a dragon or other fierce animal. Proteus is an apt symbol for Canada's major newspapers. Like Proteus, we look old and have been around for a long time. But we still have the vitality to change in response to each new difficulty. Despite tough challenges, the newspaper industry will continue to flourish because of its natural strengths and its ability to adapt. My confidence is based on the fact that we have faced adversity before and have become a stronger, more dynamic industry.

The newspaper business has responded to the advent of TV by reinventing itself. If you had asked people in the 1950s where they got their breaking news, they would have said from their daily newspapers. Our parents relaxed after dinner with their evening papers and listened to the radio. But today television broadcasts 24 hours a day and major news stories are initially reported by it—CNN being an obvious case in point. Who can forget watching the Gulf War in 1992 with actual missile strikes? Or who doesn't remember following O. J. Simpson in his white Ford Bronco as he tried to decide whether to turn himself in? Competition from television *is* intensifying. We now have not one but several 24-hour-a-day news stations.

There is no denying television's impact on newspapers. The percentage of people who read them every day has dropped dramatically from 80 percent 30 years ago to 62 percent today.

The result? Most urban centres now have only one daily newspaper. Toronto is the exception, with four thriving dailies, and a possible fifth on the horizon, which makes the city extremely fortunate in its access to different points of view. Still, while Toronto has been a wonderful print market, newspapers, in general, have suffered at the hands of television. In fact, 15 percent of the country's newspapers have shut their doors over the past 20 years, yet the newspapers that do remain continue to flourish.

The question is, then, how have the surviving daily newspapers responded so vigorously to the challenge posed by television? First, they switched their focus from the evening to the morning. Television preempted the evening time that once had been set aside for reading the paper. Those newspapers that fought this change generally lost and went out of business. At the *Toronto Star,* we know our very survival depended on switching from evening to morning publication.

That decision cost the *Star* $400 million. Let me explain why. It is essential that we get a morning paper on the reader's doorstep by 6:00 a.m. To be competitive with the *Toronto Sun,* we have to publish the results of the Toronto Blue Jays game played the night before in, say, California. The game doesn't end until 1:30 a.m. EST. That means we need a plant that can print 500,000 copies of the paper between 2:00 a.m. and 4:00 a.m. That way it reaches the subscriber by 6:00 a.m. The reality is that we start printing at 1:00 a.m., and the first papers off the presses go to areas just outside Toronto. At 2:00 a.m., we stop the presses, replate for the sports update and deliver the finished paper to our city readers by the time the ink has barely dried. My point is simple: afternoon papers are dead, we had to adapt and we did.

Our second response to the television challenge was to produce a paper with much more colour. You can't compete with colour television in black and white. Colour provides greater interest for readers and greater impact for advertisers. Even the *New York Times* has recently made the move to colour. That venerable paper took a while to follow our lead, but it took the *Globe and Mail* even longer.

The third way we responded to the challenge of television was to become more interpretive, more analytical. A paper at mid-century might have had 23 brief stories on its cover page. Today a newspaper's front page has five to seven in-depth articles.

This development toward more in-depth coverage is one that we have welcomed. It builds upon the *Star*'s tradition of fighting for social justice—a tradition that publisher John Honderich and his team are carrying on with distinction. And we believe strongly that we have made a difference. Here, in my opinion, are some of our recent successes.

- We published a groundbreaking series on spousal abuse and children at risk. This series sparked widespread public debate, prompted a formal Ontario government review and won the prestigious Michener Award for meritorious public service in journalism.

- We were among the first to argue for a megacity in Toronto, which is now a reality.

- We have reported on the shocking differences in the quality of care provided by different hospitals and doctors. We have called for more public disclosure in Ontario.
- We have highlighted youth unemployment in a series called "Lives on Hold." This series, which stimulated the federal government's interest in youth-employment programs, was nominated for a Michener Award in 1998.
- We recently investigated the taxi industry in Toronto. The *Star*'s analysis prompted a formal review of that business, as well.

The fourth and final way we responded to television was the simplest, but probably the most profound of all. We remained faithful to our traditional strengths. Each media outlet that provides news has its own virtues. Radio can be listened to while driving to and from work. Television has motion and immediacy. But newspapers have something no other medium has: they distill the news, compress it and make it accessible.

The problem with TV news is that you can't fast-forward. If the viewer is interested in the fourth story in that night's "lineup," as those in television call it, he or she has to watch the first three stories, as well.

Our second response to the television challenge was to produce a paper with much more colour.

In a newspaper, though, there might be seven headlines on the front page. Let's say you're somewhat interested in four of these. You read the first three paragraphs of these stories and, if the paper is well written, you've gotten the gist of the day's news. You have already received as much information as you would have in a 15-minute TV newscast. Let's suppose you decide to read two of the stories in greater depth. It takes about as long to do that as it likely took you to read up to this point in this essay and find out what you already know: people read newspapers with a set of choices they don't have in other media. We scan some stories and read others in-depth.

That's why today's newspaper industry is flourishing 17 years after Ted Turner's famous boast that "the newspaper, as we know it, will be dead in 10 years." Nineteen ninety-seven, in fact, was the most profitable year ever for North American newspapers.

How profitable has the industry been? Profitable enough that Conrad Black is willing to wager $150 million that he can launch a successful newspaper in Toronto. The key, for Black, will be to find a niche. Even with the resources he has at his disposal, and the size of paper he is contemplating, it will be difficult to provide a better business section than the *Globe and Mail*'s, although his recent acquisition of the *Financial Post* is a good start. Still, he will also have to publish better local news and sports sections than the *Star* and the *Sun*.

But is there room for a paper with good writing that stimulates debate? I think so. My test is: Will Black be able to create a buzz around the watercooler? Will people say, "Did you read what Black's paper said today?" If he can do that, he will have a business.

Many people will insist that television might not kill the newspaper industry, but the Internet will. In fact, a recent *Financial Post* article had the headline: "Newspapers Losing Ground as King of Classified." And the subhead read: "Internet could steal $4.1 billion in advertising by 2001." A report from Forrester Research in the United States concluded in 1997 that "Newspapers are in big trouble and they're going to get hammered."

News like that we can do without. The Internet is a wonderful new medium. It will find an important place in consumers' lives, along with other media. Yet I am confident that, while the Internet will change our business dramatically over the next 20 years, we can live with it. In fact, newspapers and the Internet will complement each other.

As more people use the Internet, there are two questions the newspaper industry must answer. What will happen to our readership and what will happen to our advertising? In both these areas, newspapers will benefit from their relationship with the Internet.

Let's consider readership first. There are three reasons readers won't forsake newspapers for the Internet. First, research has shown that people getting information on-line are not using it as a substitute for reading the newspaper. Actually, the on-line capability expands our role.

Those using the Internet can be divided into three distinct groups:

- Some look for immediacy. They want to know at 10:45 p.m. who won the hockey game. We can provide that information on the Internet, which means we are back in the business of "breaking news." We can give readers the score at 10:45 and a commentary on the game the next morning in the paper.
- Then there are those who want to study a subject in-depth. They want access to newspaper archives and are willing to pay for it through the Internet.
- And, finally, there are some people who get all their information on-line. Using services like Pointcast or Timecast, they are presented with their own customized newspaper each time they log on. Fortunately most of these people weren't regular newspaper readers. They are new customers.

The second reason the Internet won't lure newspaper readers away is that it performs different tasks. Derrick de Kerckhove, director of the McLuhan Program in Culture and Technology at the University of Toronto, states the issue well: "The job of the newspaper is to sort out items which are relevant to the public's interest, over and above those which address purely individual needs." In other words, the issues we should know about will fall through the cracks because we didn't request them—the Quebec ice storm, for example. That's why customized on-line newspapers don't work.

The reverse, however, is true for business information. I am interested in specific subject areas—the communication industry, for example—and customized reports can be waiting for me on-line when I arrive at work. That's worth paying for.

Would anyone really look forward to a Sunday morning curled up in an easy chair with a cup of coffee and a computer screen?

The final reason our readers will stay with us is the "feel" of a newspaper compared to a screen. Would anyone really look forward to a Sunday morning curled up in an easy chair with a cup of coffee and a computer screen? I don't think so. A newspaper in its present form works. It's already wonderfully interactive. You can pick it up and put it down whenever you want.

The reality is that people use the Internet during the day for business information and in the evening for personal interest, and that hour spent in the evening cuts into television viewing, not newspaper reading. Very few people are on-line over breakfast.

Now let's look at advertising, the second area of potential competition between the Internet and the press. Here again, newspapers can expand their role, particularly with respect to classified advertising. Why classified? Because it accounts for 25 percent of newspaper revenue and a higher proportion of subsequent profits.

There's not much incentive for future readers to trudge through pages of advertisements for used cars, real estate and jobs when a search engine can explore dozens of computer databases. Those who are on-line can sort complex data quickly, such as the make, price, year and model of a car. They can find a consumer report rating. They can look at houses in a desired neighbourhood. They can even take a tour inside a prospective house.

Electronic classifieds are definitely a threat. A customer can go to the Internet site, Auto-by-Tel—which has enlisted 2,200 dealers across North America—and get a quote from a dealer that participates in this buying service. In fact, in 1997 four percent of new cars were sold over the Net. What will this mean to dealerships in the long run? What will it mean to dealers' display ads? What will it mean to newspapers?

The key to the future of the newspaper industry lies in its continuing ability to bring buyers and sellers together. Newspapers have always been the gateway to classifieds. But our customers don't merely want to read print classifieds on-line; they want value-added service. We must take advantage of the interactive capability of the new delivery system and assist the buyer and seller in completing the transaction.

Partnerships will enable us to do that. Take, for example, Classified Ventures, a new on-line technology partnership that includes Times Mirror, the Tribune Company, Gannett, Knight Ridder, the New York Times Company and the Washington Post Company. This group can direct traffic to its site through in-paper promotion. Yet the scope of the consortium will attract national advertisers who will be interested in advertising on-line with the potential of millions of daily hits.

These developments and others have led Forrester Research to revisit its conclusions. They now believe that newspapers have an advantage and that classified advertising is ours to lose. At the *Toronto Star,* we don't intend to let it slip between our fingers.

The *Star* has also taken significant steps forward in on-line advertising. Our Web site, with 150,000 page views per day, is one of the busiest in Canada. If the theatre interests you, you can check out what the critics have said and then order tickets. If you want to dine out after the performance, our site can show you the possibilities within easy walking distance. If you want to read the reviews of a particular restaurant or look over the menu, just double-click. You can even use e-mail to book a table for Saturday night.

And all this valuable information is free. It's like having a private concierge at home. In short, we see the Internet as a means of building our franchise.

Edmund Burke once wrote: "You can rarely plan the future by the past." Newspapers are entering an uncertain time, but they will continue to prosper in the years ahead because of their natural strengths and their ability to adapt. Perhaps if the industry emulates Proteus and changes its shape as the situation demands, it will flourish in the 21st century and beyond.

This article has been adapted from a speech given by David Galloway at the Canadian Club in Toronto in April 1998.

HILARY BROWN

Hilary Brown was often the first and the only female to have a salaried job in her particular field. Her firsts include female network announcer on the CBC (1968); TV reporter on Parliament Hill in Ottawa (1970); network foreign news reporter for ABC News, based in London and then Paris (1973-77); TV correspondent for NBC News in Tel Aviv, Israel (1977-80); and U.S. Pentagon correspondent for NBC News (1980-81).

Brown covered many of the major conflicts overseas for ABC and NBC News for the better part of 25 years, with the exception of seven years in Toronto as a television news anchor. She has reported from every country in the world except Australia, and has covered at least 10 wars, from the Indo-Pakistan conflict of 1971 to the Bosnian war in the 1990s. She was one of the last correspondents to be helicoptered out of Vietnam at the fall of Saigon in April 1975.

Keeping Your Head Down on the Firing Line

I HAVE OFTEN THOUGHT that foreign correspondents are like cats: they've got nine lives and most use up five or six before they retire or take up teaching. Many, of course, use them all up and die with their boots on. I imagine that I would like to peg out that way, if only because I don't think I could teach anybody anything. I'm also strangely influenced by that famously snide comment by George Bernard Shaw: "He who can, does. He who cannot, teaches."

After more than 25 years on the road as a TV news reporter, mainly working for ABC, I would say that I have used up at least seven of those nine lives, and possibly an equal number of half-lives. Most of the time it's been my fault. People used to say, "Hilary Brown doesn't know the meaning of fear." To which I would add: "Yes, it's one of the many words I don't know the meaning of." I can't honestly say that I have ever learned a thing from experience; I have simply found yet another, original way to make myself a casualty. My capacity for error is almost limitless.

One of the best examples of this tendency was in Iran during the revolution in 1979. In November of that year, Iranian "students" seized the U.S. embassy in Tehran and took 65 Americans hostage. The entire Western press corps descended on Tehran, and for weeks Iran became a kind of domestic story for the U.S. networks.

We covered everything, including a sudden coup d'état in the northwest of the country in a town called Tabriz, near the Turkish border. Tens of thousands of Turkish-speaking Iranians took to the streets and started rioting in favour of autonomy. At least I think that's what they were shouting about.

I immediately flew up there with my camera crew and we hit the ground running, taking only a few minutes to check into the only Western-style hotel in town before rushing out to cover the action. The mob had marched on the radio and TV stations and taken control of both. We took pictures of that. Having just read Edward Luttwak's manual *Coup d'état,* I then had the bright idea that we should check out the governor's house.

At the time, I was wearing a white trench coat over dark trousers, with no head scarf. About 5,000 people had surrounded the building, and we plunged into the crowd. The soundman was linked to the cameraman with his video cable; and because it was getting dark, I was linked to the soundman by a hand light plugged into his battery pack. Within seconds I was separated from my crew by this surging, screaming, all-male mob, which began to maul me. I felt that every hand in Tabriz was on some part of my body. The crew couldn't reach me as I was carried farther and farther away from them by this suffocating sea of screaming, swarthy men.

I was quite sure they were going to tear me limb from limb and felt not so much fear as intense shame that I had so completely misread the situation, that I had rushed into that volatile, excitable crowd without a second thought, and that I had endangered all of our lives, not just my own. To make matters worse, I was wearing a white coat, which stood out like a beacon. Why wasn't I wearing dark clothing and a head scarf? I was a blonde, for God's sake.

And suddenly, as quickly as the mob had closed around me, it parted again and let me go.

I also thought intensely of my family, of my husband, John Bierman, and our new son, Jonathan, then only four months old, and how wrong I had been to leave them—against my husband's advice—to cover what he said was a dangerous news story. As a BBC correspondent who was the first reporter into Tehran after the seizure of the American embassy, he knew what he was talking about.

No one, not even an armed force, can rescue you from a hysterical mob. The only thing that can save you is the mob itself. I had lived in Iran with my husband in the early 1970s, when he was working for the BBC World Service, and suddenly every word of Farsi I'd ever learned, every polite, stylized expression, every peasant blessing, every phrase I had memorized in Farsi class somehow came tumbling out of my mouth.

And suddenly, as quickly as the mob had closed around me, it parted again and let me go. I found the crew, we got into the car, drove back to the hotel and practised rooftop journalism for the rest of the night. But not before we had earmarked a hiding place to retreat to should the mob, which by then had filled almost every street in town, break through the hotel's locked iron gates.

It didn't, and we survived the night unscathed. But how can a person be so stupid? It's partly because you're not thinking about your personal safety at such times. You're thinking about the *story* and whether you're going to get beaten by the opposition. Usually you're worried sick that you *are* being beaten. But this time our network was alone at the Tabriz insurrection, and our corporate masters in New York City were very glad to have our exclusive reports.

I am convinced that this is one of the things that drives a person to commit these greater acts of insanity. In Zaire in 1977, for example, the Western press corps was penned up at the Intercontinental Hotel in Kinshasa and confined to the capital and its outskirts while a secessionist war was being waged in the province of Shaba, formerly known as Katanga.

All air and road links, except for military traffic, had been cut to the province. I was wildly impatient to get down there and had heard an awful rumour that CBS had already made it, so I did something really quite wild. I got hold of three sets of army fatigues, talked my crew into putting them on, and at three o'clock in the morning we drove to the military airport in Kinshasa and literally stowed away on one of the military transport planes that had its engines running.

The pilot was smoking something that did not smell like tobacco, and his cargo was several hundred cans of gasoline. By some miracle, we took off and landed without exploding into a fireball, and several hours later we were busy filming everything that moved in Shaba province. I don't remember worrying about the utter folly of all this: apart from the risk of being blown up, we could quite easily have been arrested and spent the next few years rotting in jail. I remember thinking, Thank God we're competitive on this story.

I still have the army fatigues as a souvenir. That's not nearly as original as the souvenir secured by a correspondent for the *New York Times,* who swiped a large sign posted next to the Intercontinental Hotel swimming pool that read: It Is Absolutely Forbidden to Picnic on the Grass, Piss in the Pool or Come with Animals.

There were stories where you *ought* to have been killed by shot and shell but actually came closest to meeting your maker when you were doing something utterly ordinary, such as tripping on the stairs or slipping in the bath. (I've done both, of course, being six feet tall in shoes and the world's clumsiest woman.) That was the case for me in Bosnia in the late winter of 1993, when the Serbs were engaged in their loathsome campaign of "ethnic cleansing" in the eastern part of the country.

Ethnic cleansing meant making an area pure for Serbs by driving out its unarmed, non-Serb civilians by force, including murder, rape, torture and pillage. ABC News wanted to put a satellite dish into the northern town of Tuzla to feed material from Srebenica and other points of refuge in Bosnian-held territory.

We were a small team of seven—a producer, engineer, cameraman, soundman, correspondent, translator and logistics producer—driving in a Bedford truck, an armour-plated Land Rover and a tiny but unstoppable Lada. Armed with walkie-talkies to communicate with one another, we carried all our supplies, including food, gasoline, generators, satellite phones, bedding and a large supply of tapes and camera gear. Our instructions were to take our dish from Split, on the Croatian coast, through Herzegovina and over the Bosnian mountains to Tuzla. That's about 100 miles. It took us four days.

The main highway was too dangerous—the two sides were fighting for control of it and shelled anything that moved—so we had to take the back roads through the mountains. These were unploughed logging trails covered in deep snow, which meant we had no idea how wide the trail actually was and where the ditch began. Sometimes the trail simply fell away on one side into a steep, heart-stopping ravine. And throughout the journey we kept passing the wrecks of other trucks and even U.N. armoured personnel carriers that had gone over the side.

We figured we'd probably either freeze to death in an attempt to walk through deep snow to the nearest village, since we hadn't seen one for miles, or we'd freeze to death huddled together in our little convoy.

On Day One, our engineer, Ken Suckling, who was driving the Bedford, suddenly came on the two-way radio and shouted, "I'm outta control. I'm outta control!" as the truck, loaded with satellite gear, went into a skid on a steep descent and thundered down the mountain track to what we thought was certain death for him and Elvis, our young translator. Our Australian camera team—Niki Millard and Matt Logan—were in front in the Lada, listening to an Elvis Presley tape at full volume. "Suddenly all we could see in the rearview mirror were the whites of Ken's eyes," Niki said later. Somehow Ken managed to turn into the skid and shudder to a stop at the bottom of the hill.

From that point on, we hooked the steel cable on the front of the Land Rover onto the rear bumper of the truck going downhill and towed the truck going up. This worked well until we hit a long, flat, wooded stretch of road beside a river that ran for miles, without any sign of life at all, on or off the track.

In the late afternoon of Day Two, the Land Rover broke down in bone-chilling cold. Each one of us silently calculated the odds of survival if we didn't get the thing going within a few hours. We figured we'd probably either freeze to death in an attempt to walk through deep snow to the nearest village, since we hadn't seen one for miles, or we'd freeze to death huddled together in our little convoy. Fortunately Ken and the logistics man, David Mills, were former servicemen in the British army, and they got the Land Rover going again.

On Day Three, under clear blue skies and in achingly beautiful mountain country, the Land Rover, top-heavy with its armour-plating, suddenly slithered off the road and onto a sloping soft shoulder and went into an unforgettable slow-motion roll. David was at the wheel, I was in the passenger seat and our producer, Marcus Wilford, was in the back. Somehow the distribution of weight in the vehicle stopped us as we were about to flip over, and just as I had finished composing in my mind the headline that might appear in my hometown paper: "Canadian News Hen Buried with TV Team in Armour-Plated Tomb in Bosnian Snowdrift—No Survivors."

We hung in what felt like midair, though, and then managed to crawl out through the passenger door. David coolly pulled out the steel cable, wrapped it around a tree, hooked it back onto the Land Rover, crawled back into the vehicle, turned it on and *winched* the thing out of the snowdrift and onto the road again.

By comparison, Day Four was really uneventful: we hit a major snowstorm but attached ourselves to an awesomely efficient Dutch U.N. engineering platoon assigned to clear the road. If any vehicle was blocking the route, the soldiers either winched it out, or if that wasn't possible, they'd push it over the side, having invited the occupants to get out. If a ditch made the road impassable, they cut down several trees and built a bridge over it. So our U.N. platoon escorted us into Tuzla along the final stretch—20 miles of paved road, known as Bomb Alley because it was within firing range of Serb guns. The trick was to put on your bulletproof vest, say a prayer, and take it at speed, which we did.

In the two subsequent years of the Bosnian war, I suppose we ran many risks on our tours of duty. Merely driving down Sniper Alley in Sarajevo, between the TV station and the Holiday Inn every day, was slightly unnerving, though we were protected by armour-plated cars and bulletproof vests. And getting caught in the middle of a mortar attack, which happened to us in central Bosnia, concentrated our minds most wonderfully. But I certainly used up at least one life on that drive from Split to Tuzla in the winter of 1993. Our first report that year on ABC's *World News Tonight* was about the trip—a rare departure from the network's policy of *not* broadcasting how reporters actually do their jobs.

That kind of journalism—how journalists get or don't get their stories—brings to mind another hellhole where I used up one or two more lives. That was El Salvador in the early 1980s, during the long and bitter war between leftist guerrillas and the U.S.-backed government. Often the guerrillas would come right into the cities to harry government forces.

Trying to cover such a war for television was extremely dangerous, mainly because there *was* no front line. You didn't know where the guerrillas were, and the fact was, they were everywhere. This situation made it very easy to get caught in a crossfire, which happened to the distinguished British reporter David Blundy, who died of his wounds as a result. His last words were: "Get me out of here." We had his fate in mind every time we had to do a piece to camera, known in the trade as a "standup." In El Salvador, a standup was usually done lying down in one take.

The other great risk was in the countryside, crossing the no-man's-land between areas under government control and those held by rebels. Journalists often did so to meet and talk with the rebels, but this was highly dangerous if you were caught either by government soldiers or armed "vigilantes," who usually drove around in the back of pickup trucks. During my assignment in El Salvador, a team of Dutch journalists made an assignation with a group of rebels and were murdered by the Treasury Police in a hail of machine-gun fire.

I immediately thought, This is it.
They're vigilantes. We've had it.

But our rendezvous with the rebels happened a few days before that atrocity. From one of the nongovernmental agencies, we had gotten wind of a massacre, allegedly by government troops, of most of the inhabitants of a village about 40 miles from the capital of San Salvador. We thought we were slightly ahead of the rest of the press pack—San Salvador was stiff with journalists at the time—and rushed out to find the village. This was my first assignment in El Salvador (though my seventh or eighth war), and I was with a an experienced Mexican TV crew often used by ABC.

We reached the side road leading down to the village and found a small group of journalists—maybe three or four—but to my relief, no other TV team. These journalists had heard about the massacre, too, but they were hesitating because they thought it was too dangerous to go down the road. I looked at the crew and said, "It's your call, guys. You know this place and I don't." They agreed to go, so we started out on foot.

After a few minutes, a voice behind us called out, "Wait for me!" It was a woman named Joanne Omang, who had bad teeth and a weight problem and who at the time was writing a clever little column for the *Washington Post* about the press corps in El Salvador. She wanted to walk in with us and, against my better judgement, we let her. We could hardly stop her, anyway.

After about a mile, we came into a clearing, and suddenly two or three rebels stood up in the long grass. Wild-eyed, they pointed their guns at us. The crew identified itself—and us—and stated our mission. The rebels relaxed and said they'd take us to their leader. (Yes, people actually *do* say that.)

We met well outside the village, had a long chat in Spanish, and for reasons I didn't quite understand (I know only French and could follow very little of the conversation), we agreed that we would come back the following morning at an appointed time. Then we started the walk back through the no-man's-land.

The crew and I set a pretty brisk pace, all of us quite aware of the danger except, it seemed, Ms. Omang. She was unable to keep up the pace, so we had to stop and let her sit and catch her breath. As we rounded a bend in the road, a pickup truck with four or five men in the back came into view. I immediately thought, This is it. They're vigilantes. We've had it. But they were merely bringing supplies to the rebels. So, after a few more rest stops for Ms. Omang, we eventually made it back to the main road and then to the capital. At the hotel where all the press was staying, we arranged to return the following morning.

Later that evening, though, the Mexican crew members drew our producer aside and said they weren't happy about going back with a woman, especially two women. They thought it was too dangerous, particularly since one of the women was out of shape and couldn't walk any distance at speed.

Then our news requirements for the following day changed: ABC's Sunday morning show with David Brinkley wanted me to do a short report and two-way live talk from San Salvador. So I couldn't return to the rebel camp, anyway. This development made it easier to tell Ms. Omang that our crew would go in alone. I found her in the hotel bar and told her about the situation. Her response was clear enough: "Fuck you, sister." I think I might have suggested she try the same thing herself. Then I returned to our office to work, telling myself I should have known better than to pick up a hitchhiker.

Several months later, the *Washington Journalism Review* published an issue devoted to women in war. Ms. Omang was on the cover, and inside was a clever little first-person piece about working in El Salvador that she had written. It included a paragraph about meeting the rebels with an ABC crew and its correspondent, Hilary Brown. She wrote that I didn't go back the second day. According to her, I preferred to leave the reporting to her crew.

I have many faults, but not even my enemies would say that cowardice is one of them. The public-relations officer at ABC didn't think the article was worth getting upset about, not having an enormous amount of respect for the *Washington Journalism Review.* I thought I should at least write a letter to the editor, setting out my recollection of events. But then an Israeli diplomat was shot in London, Israel launched an invasion of Lebanon, and I had to jump on a plane to cover that little war—my ninth, I believe.

I don't think I used up any lives in Israel on that assignment, or at any other time there. (I was based in Tel Aviv for NBC News between 1977 and 1980 and have been rotated in and out of Israel dozens of times for ABC.) But

I did crash through a crossing point on the Israeli-Lebanese border in a car at about 4:30 a.m. The Israelis weren't letting journalists cross the border, and I knew that CBS had managed to get into Lebanon. I just *had* to get in there, too.

The best time to attempt this, I thought, was very early in the morning—the "hour of the wolf," when a person's resistance is at its lowest ebb and when the border guards might even be half asleep. I knew about a small crossing point on the crest of a hill. The road paralleled the actual border so that you could do a right turn and drive into Lebanon.

The guard post was on the left side of the road, a few yards away from the barrier, which made it ideal. Although we had a driver, I insisted on taking the wheel, and as we approached the crossing point, I put my foot on the gas, roared past the guard into a right turn, knocked the low metal barrier aside and sped into Lebanon. Normally you can expect the guards to shoot at your wheels, but I think they were too sleepy or too surprised to react. My crew and driver were absolutely silent through the entire adventure, but they did do a lot of heavy breathing.

Where else have I used up a life? Perhaps in Vietnam at the fall of Saigon in April 1975. We were on one of the last helicopters to lift off the roof of the U.S. embassy, and most of those flights, we were told, took enemy fire. But we landed safely on the American aircraft carrier USS *Hancock,* as did every single chopper carrying civilians during that extraordinary evacuation from Saigon, the greatest single movement of people during that war.

Perhaps I lost another life in Cyprus during the Turkish invasion in July 1974. I managed to seize a U.N. vehicle abandoned by its Austrian crew, which had been considerate enough to leave the keys. We used it to drive back and forth across the so-called Green Line between the Greek and Turkish sides. After we shot film of the invasion, we drove back across the border to the Greek side and shipped the footage out to London, England.

Most of the press corps members were at the Ledra Palace Hotel, right on the line, where a fairly lively firefight raged between Greek Cypriot National Guards and Turkish Cypriot fighters. I continued to drive back and forth in front of the hotel until Ron Ben-Ishai, a very experienced Israeli military correspondent with the former rank of colonel in his country's defence force, stopped me and said quietly in his almost perfect English: "Heelary, don't do that. The are not shooting at each other anymore. They are shooting at *you.*"

Or perhaps I forfeited a life in the Sudan in 1998, covering the terrible famine that descended on the people in the southern part of the country through a combination of drought and 15 years of civil war. Southern Sudan is one of the more remote places on the planet, as well as being one of the most godforsaken. In the dry season, the land is a sun-baked, windswept, half-empty desert. The airstrips are rough lines in the sand, barely visible from above. To get there you have to fly from Nairobi in a single-engine plane for seven hours, then refuel in the border hamlet of Lokochokio. With only one pilot, and overloaded with camera gear. I don't mind admitting that I flew in there with all fingers on both hands crossed, and with various lucky charms in various pockets of my safari jacket.

But then you consider the state of the people of southern Sudan, these walking skeletons who have walked for three, four, sometimes seven days to get to the landing strip where they know there's a feeding centre and a handful of corn. That's what the food ration worked out to when we were there: one cup of corn per person per week. The people lived on roots and leaves; they even ransacked anthills for the scraps of food stored by the insects. When you consider their plight, you feel pretty ashamed of your own fears about single-engine planes and tricky airstrips.

At one point during my career, though, my attitude toward the inherent risks of my occupation changed. As a mother, it's a terrible wrench to leave your child to go off on a long and difficult assignment, and you often ask yourself, as a parent, if it's the responsible thing to be doing. That was one of the reasons I decided to take an anchor job for CBC-TV in Toronto in 1984, when my son was four. I had calculated that in the previous year I'd been on the road for about 80 percent of the time. I felt it wasn't fair to him or to my husband. I have since defined anchoring as "death by hair spray," but for seven years I came home every night in one piece.

Now our son is grown to the alarming height of six foot seven. He is quite independent and, in many ways, much more mature than I am, though he's only 18. And my husband, who now writes wonderful, immensely readable biographies, is probably glad to have me back on the road again, out of his hair. He still dedicates his books to me, though I feel that what he'd really like to say is: "To Hilary, without whose help this book would have been finished three years ago."

JONATHAN MANTHORPE

Jonathan Manthorpe is the international-affairs columnist for the *Vancouver Sun*. He concentrates on events in Asia, and his columns are published throughout the Southam group of newspapers. Manthorpe was the Southam News Asia correspondent for five years until the end of 1997 when the Hong Kong bureau was closed.

From 1989 until 1993, Manthorpe was the Southam News correspondent in sub-Saharan Africa, a territory that included 35 countries, 17 wars and five famines at the time. Manthorpe joined Southam News as European correspondent in 1984. He was working from Britain as a freelancer after two years as a special adviser to Prime Minister Pierre Elliott Trudeau on patriation of the Canadian Constitution.

Manthorpe went to Europe as the *Toronto Star*'s bureau chief in 1979 after nearly 10 years as a reporter and columnist on Canadian politics for the *Star* and the *Globe and Mail*.

The Decline of Foreign News in Canada's Media

IT IS A PARADOX of modern journalism that as the revolution in information technology has made the corners of the world more and more accessible, the presentation of news has become increasingly parochial. At least this is certainly the case with most of what has come to be regarded in the past quarter century or so as the mainstream media: metropolitan daily newspapers and national television and radio stations. Many of the big-city dailies in Canada can now go for days without a foreign story on the front page, and it is very common to hear and watch broadcasts with no international news until after the commercial break.

The reasons for this phenomenon are many and varied. They differ from country to country, and some buck the trend. Newspapers in Hong Kong, for example, carry considerable amounts of regional and international news in all sections, which indicates the overriding influence on newspaper content. Journalism is a reflection of the society in which it operates. A mercantile centre like Hong Kong that lives on its wits needs to know and understand the world around it.

Canada, on the other hand, can afford to live in isolated self-absorption. The relative lack of interest in international affairs in Canadian newspapers merely mirrors the attitude of society as a whole. Canada has only one vital international relationship and that is with the United States. Despite decades of fretting and worrying by a succession of governments, Canada has never produced an independent foreign policy or individual view of the world worthy of distinction. By largely ignoring the world around it, Canadian media do no more than cater to the view of society at large.

Within Canadian journalism, the question of international news coverage is only occasionally an issue. The positions and arguments put forward frequently stem, inevitably, from the spot on the information network where the speaker is standing. Here's the rub. The revolution in information technology has not only thrown the industry into a turmoil of squabbling and reevaluation about which medium is best able to carry the different types of news, it has also made it very hard for any one analyst to stand far enough back to get the whole beast in focus.

Much pontification, and this is especially true of newspapers, is based on a very narrow view of the animal in question, much as palaeontologists speculate about the habits and lifestyles of dinosaurs based on one fossilized foot bone. A restricted view makes it very easy to ask the wrong questions. The question, surely, should be whether the general public has available to it all the information about the world around it that it wants and needs.

The answer cannot be anything other than yes, it does. But in the past 25 years or so the sources of that information have changed and increased dramatically to the point where it is no longer sensible to imagine that a large daily newspaper or a network television station can or should try to provide the kind of one-stop information service that has traditionally been the case. The explosion of specialized magazines, periodicals and, indeed, newspapers in recent years, as well as the seemingly endless scroll of one-topic channels on television and, of course, the limitless strands of the Internet, suggest that there are now only niche markets. International affairs has become more like gardening, weight lifting and bird watching—a topic for aficionados.

Newspapers have been scrambling to redefine themselves since the mid-1970s when television began to fully appreciate and use the edge its technology gave it to present news and dominate the daily public agenda. The initial fear in newspapers that the printed word would become irrelevant in the electronic age has now been largely discounted. Newspapers have not only survived but prospered. Many papers in Canada have done this by filling their pages with local issues and concerns with a detail television cannot match. This tendency has frequently been to the detriment of national and international coverage.

Some tabloids, particularly in countries such as the United Kingdom, have become little more than daily commentaries on the entertainment and celebrity industries. The *Sun* in London, England, is a good example of a publication that has beaten television's usurpation of news presentation by writing to an astonishing extent about the people who inhabit the television world. It has developed a bizarre symbiotic relationship whereby the *Sun* can make and break—it has developed a format for doing both—the television personalities on which it feeds.

As newspapers have gained more confidence in their survival, many have begun to perceive the shape of a future concentrating on analysis, explanation and exploration of events and issues. This realization is undoubtedly the right track, for the moment at least. Whether the Internet will eventually make obsolete the whole notion of communicating by making marks on dead trees is currently unknowable. However, there are suggestions that in the immediate future classic television has more to fear from the Internet than do newspapers and magazines.

In early 1998, the U.S. investment bank Hambrecht and Quist conducted a survey of 100,000 Internet users. The survey found that 25 percent said they watched less television because of the Internet while only 14 percent said they read less as a result of Internet use. Sixty percent said the Internet made no difference to their consumption of information from other media. So we are at the moment in the midst of a straggling revolution for which, by the competitive nature of the business and its multiplicity of audiences, there can be no dominating vision or unifying marching song.

Coverage of foreign affairs is not a major component on anybody's blueprints for what the new age of newspapers should deal with or look like. A case in point is the new national newspaper due to be produced in the fall of 1998 by Conrad Black's Southam organization. People involved in the planning say a strategy for reporting international affairs has hardly figured in the preparations. This seeming omission is undoubtedly partly explained by the wide range of foreign news sources the new paper will have available to it, including Black's London *Daily Telegraph* and the remaining Southam foreign bureaus. Foreign coverage is not a problem the planners of the new paper need to confront. It will take care of itself.

Some tabloids, particularly in countries such as the United Kingdom, have become little more than daily commentaries on the entertainment and celebrity industries.

That is also symbolic of the general sense, especially in Canada, that a daily dose of news about world affairs is no longer an essential vitamin in the life of an educated and informed person. It has become in some quarters chic and almost an article of faith that it is possible to live a rich, fulfilled and sophisticated life while cultivating ignorance about events in the wider world. I have heard a book editor, still recovering from the dismal sales of a rather good book by a former foreign correspondent, complain that "Canadians just aren't interested in foreign stuff."

This feeling is reflected in the low status foreign correspondents and foreign editors have traditionally had in Canadian newspapers. It is unusual to find a Canadian paper with a proper foreign editor who is anything more than the fitter of wire copy into the space left over when other section editors have made their bids. To find a foreign editor who actually has experience as a correspondent is even rarer. While in Britain or the United States it would generally be felt that foreign-corresponding experience is necessary among the qualifications for a senior editorial post, in Canada it is very unusual to find a senior editor who has done anything but diligently work up the ladder of domestic office politics. Canadian newspapers in general are bad at using the foreign correspondents they do have and even worse at integrating them back into the hierarchy at home.

If anything, the low status afforded foreign correspondents and international news has intensified in recent years. City editors, consumed by their competition with the local electronic media and convinced theirs is the only critical battle for newspaper survival, tend to regard foreign news as an unnecessary frill. National and city editors can also be quite vitriolic in the internal battles for scarce financial resources. Short-staffed domestic editors become outlandishly outraged at the budget for a foreign bureau that might represent the cost of three or four street reporters the editor doesn't have. I remember a few years ago touring most of the large Southam newspapers to try to explain the importance of Asian news coverage to editors. There was only one question that came up consistently and that was how much it cost to keep me in Hong Kong.

Given the choice between a crackerjack foreign story and a mediocre domestic tale that may ingratiate the newspaper with its readers, the local story will win every time.

Domestic editors have conclusively won the arguments about allocation of newspaper resources in recent years. For example, my own organization, Southam News, which provides copy to all daily papers owned by Southam, had probably the largest networks of foreign bureaus of any Canadian news outlet a decade ago. There were staff correspondents in London, Washington, Costa Rica, Moscow, Cairo, Harare and Hong Kong. But the past decade has seen progressive cutbacks as editors questioned whether public interest in foreign affairs justified the investment in those bureaus.

First, the Latin American bureau was closed and then, after the transition to a democratic government in South Africa in 1993, the African base in Zimbabwe was dispensed with. When Conrad Black obtained complete control of Southam in 1996, the process was accelerated. It was argued that it was wasteful and unnecessary to duplicate offices in regions where Black already had bureaus through his other newspaper holdings, especially the *Daily Telegraph.* It made more economic sense, the argument went, to make *Telegraph* copy available to the Southam papers than to operate a separate, vastly expensive network. The closure of Southam's Moscow and Middle East bureaus quickly followed, and in 1997 the office in Hong Kong was shut down.

I must admit to deep personal prejudice on this last closure since I was the correspondent charged with turning out the lights. Canadians are the largest minority in Hong Kong. The 200,000 Canadians in the city state form a population concentration on a par with medium-size cities back home such as Regina, Victoria and Windsor, where Southam has newspapers. In addition, there are some 500,000 people in Hong Kong who have the right to apply for Canadian residency through family links. What happens in Hong Kong, and by extension China, is a domestic story for Canada. While *Telegraph* correspondents are generally quite good reporters, it would be unfair and unrealistic to expect them to show much sympathy, understanding or passion for reporting Canada's special links with Asia. A very large proportion of the Canadian newspaper-reading public has therefore lost direct touch with one of the few places in the world outside the United States where it can be justifiably claimed that Canada has a direct and continuing interest.

Foreign correspondents, of course, bewail the closure of foreign bureaus and the dearth of international news and analysis in their papers. They frequently speak sniffily about a deplorable dumbing-down of Canadian public affairs and debate. They may also worry eloquently about increasing dependence on non-Canadian sources for news, whether it is reliance on wire services such as British Reuters and the U.S. Associated Press or syndicated copy circulated by newspapers such as the *New York Times* and the *Washington Post* and London newspapers such as the *Times,* the *Daily Telegraph* and *the Guardian.*

Where, ask the embattled foreign correspondents, is the Canadian view of the world? Senior editors often put foreign news high on their list of priorities for their newspapers and speak fulsomely of the rounded character and gravitas it gives their publications. But they ruefully admit that when it actually comes down to the dirty daily business of putting the paper together, foreign news drops to the bottom of the list of essential content. Given the choice between a crackerjack foreign story and a mediocre domestic tale that may ingratiate the newspaper with its readers, the local story will win every time. There is a similar gap between desire and performance among readers. While surveys find that most readers place foreign news high on the list of information they want from a newspaper, analysis of what they actually read shows their eyes usually flit over international stories with hardly a pause.

The results of this turmoil are easily seen. Take, for example, the front pages of Canada's leading broadsheet newspapers on an average day, Thursday, July 9, 1998. Unrest in Nigeria following the death of imprisoned opposition leader Moshood Abiola was the main foreign story of the day chosen by those papers that put international affairs on the front page. None of the newspapers, of course, had their own correspondent at the scene. The story was helped up front in the *Globe and Mail*, the *Vancouver Sun*, the *Toronto Star* and the *Montreal Gazette*, however, by reports that a Canadian doctor, the chief coroner of Ontario, was flying to Nigeria to help verify that Abiola died of natural causes.

Other front-page foreign stories got a similar local-angle boost. The *Calgary Herald*'s only front-page foreign news dealt with the anguish of a local Croatian immigrant over his national team's defeat by France in the World Cup. The *Gazette* also put the World Cup on the front, but with the emphasis on France making it to the final, which might be considered a local angle in Quebec. As well as the Nigeria story, the *Toronto Star* front page had a report of a trial in Florida of a man alleged to have murdered a young tourist from Belleville in southern Ontario, which is within the paper's circulation area.

The *Globe and Mail*, launching a redesigned paper with its first colour pictures, had the most foreign coverage on the front page. As well as its report from Nigeria, it had a story on the threats to the peace process in Northern Ireland and four one-paragraph briefs in the expanded index column pointing to stories inside. Among the major national dailies, the *Ottawa Citizen* confirmed its reputation for hewing its own path through the forest of news judgement. Its only front-page foreign story was a report that DNA testing has confirmed a Jewish priestly family are, as has long been suspected (and, indeed, written about), descended from the prophet Moses' older brother Aaron.

Similar snapshots of the state of importance given to international affairs by Canada's major newspapers could be taken most days of the week. It is not unusual for the picture to be even more dramatic and for many of the same newspapers to go several days without a foreign story making it to the front at all. At the same time, the amount of space devoted to foreign news inside the papers is shrinking. This is not a Canadian malaise alone—if indeed a reflection of public sentiment can be described as a malaise. The *Economist*, itself a fine example of niche market prosperity, began a recent editorial on the increasing trivialization of news in newspapers with the following picture:

> On a typical day in 1898, the *Times* of London led with its usual front page of advertisements; it then carried a page reviewing some recent novels; and then acres of coverage of the Balkan war. Altogether, the newspaper had nineteen columns of foreign news, eight columns of domestic news and three about salmon fishing.

> Exactly fifty years later, the front page still carried advertisements and the leaders commented on Italy, Canada, China and the crisis in Western civilization. No change there, then.
>
> By 1998, the advertisements on the front page had been replaced by articles. There were six of them and only one was foreign; it was about Leonardo DiCaprio's new girlfriend.

The *Economist* went on to argue that the presentation of news in general is moving away from foreign affairs toward domestic concerns and from politics toward human-interest stories. It set out, deftly avoiding any comment, the argument that the modern generation of voters is therefore becoming increasingly less intelligently informed on public affairs and less able to make sound judgements. The capacity to properly direct politicians and maintain a vibrant democracy can be argued, therefore, to be at risk. The lack of foreign news in today's newspapers is a measure of world peace since the end of the Cold War, the *Economist* concluded.

That is far too simple an explanation. One of the reasons why the *Times* of 1898 carried far more foreign than domestic news was that Britain was the preeminent imperial power of the time. Everything that happened in the world impinged on British interests in some way or another. That is no longer the case. Britain's foreign interests are increasingly dominated by its relationship with Europe. The stable of foreign correspondents maintained by British newspapers in the wider world therefore keeps shrinking. More and more British papers use wire services or freelancers as the mainstay of their foreign coverage. The major "quality" London papers do keep a worldwide network of staff correspondents, but even here there are signs of wavering enthusiasm. The *Daily Telegraph*, for example, closed its Hong Kong bureau, which also covered China, after Britain returned control of the territory to Beijing on July 1, 1997. A measure of how compelling the newspaper finds the China story is that it was not until mid-1998 that the *Telegraph* appointed a new China correspondent, who will not take up his post in Beijing until later in 1998.

A nation's essential international interests are the vital determiner of how avidly newspapers cover foreign affairs. If Britain's passion for things foreign has declined with the empire, the reverse is true in the United States, the only current great imperial power. Like the Britain of 100 years ago, everything that happens in the world has some impact on U.S. interests, and coverage and staffing by the major newspapers such as the *New York Times*, the *Washington Post* and the *Wall Street Journal* reflect that. Where even the most prosperous and diligent of Western newspapers might think themselves lucky to have one correspondent in a region such as Asia or Africa, the *New York Times* and the *Post* have as many as three, each backed up with the lavish accoutrements of superpower emissaries such as prime address offices, the latest technological wizardry and research assistants fluent in the local languages.

Through this porthole of essential national interest one can look at the arid shoreline of Canadian foreign news coverage and muse that it probably justly reflects the reality of national interest. It is a continuing parlour game of Canadian public life to try to raise from the spirit world a unique view of global affairs and a special role to bring to the international community. But the harsh bottom line is that no convincing, distinctly Canadian view of the world has ever been produced. There is one vital international relationship in Canadian foreign affairs and that is with the United States. On Ottawa's relationship with Washington depend not only Canada's territorial integrity—Canada gave up any illusions of being able to defend itself decades ago—but also the overwhelming portion of its economic well-being through the largest trading partnership in the world. To a much lesser extent, Canada continues to have residual interests with Europe through history, culture, trade and its involvement in organizations such as NATO. But in the end it is only the relationship with Washington that counts.

The dalliance with Cuba, for example, is a prime example of annoying the United States for no good reason other than petulance.

Successive Canadian governments have chaffed at this reality and prodded its edges to try to create a distinctive international identity. It is easy, however, to be cynical about these efforts. The dalliance with Cuba, for example, is a prime example of annoying the United States for no good reason other than petulance. No amount of strutting by Ottawa politicians can make the Cuba play look like anything other than an afternoon flirtation by a kept woman trying to excite the attention of her bankrolling paramour.

Persistent involvement in U.N. peacekeeping operations is the most familiar and consistent attempt to develop a life outside the Ottawa-Washington corridor. Dedication to international development aid has been another area of Canadian concentration, and there has always been an imperative to speak loudly in organizations in which the United States is not a member, such as the Commonwealth and La Francophonie. Canadian journalism has tended to follow these stories, and the investment Canadian newspapers made in foreign coverage reflected a serious acceptance of these issues. Southam News and the two big Toronto daily newspapers, the *Globe and Mail* and the *Star,* kept bureaus in Africa, for example, while Canada was in the forefront of promoting development aid to the continent and was a leader of the Commonwealth's efforts to end apartheid in South Africa. Once those imperatives ended, Canadian newspapers packed up and left.

The retreat from Africa is just one example of what has become a general pulling in of journalistic horns in recent years, a reflection of popular lack of interest in the world outside and a feeling that Canada has no particular role to play. Indeed, the public and the government have not yet assimilated or come to terms with the acutely embarrassing and damaging affronts to national self-esteem delivered by the isolated high-profile problems of peacekeeping forces in Somalia, Bosnia and Rwanda. It has been said frequently that it makes no sense for a dedication to peacekeeping to be a central plank in a national defence and foreign policy. If there is peace, there is no need for peacekeepers; and if there is no peace, the international community remains unwilling to allow it to be imposed.

Traditional modes of development assistance have finally been exposed as a gross misuse of public funds that do little to help the lot of ordinary people in benighted countries and only promote corruption and the entrenchment of autocrats in power. Since the coming of democracy to South Africa, the Commonwealth has found little to excite it. Human rights in Nigeria do not inflame the same kind of passions. La Francophonie has only ever been a piece of French chauvinism in which Canada has taken part merely to scotch grandstanding by Quebec.

The present federal government's emphasis on trade and business in its foreign policy to the exclusion of almost all other considerations has had an additional, heavily dampening effect on both the public and the journalistic interest in foreign affairs. A famous Canadian editor once told a young reporter, confused about the significance of a story, "You must always remember, most businessmen are stupid." The generous interpretation of what the editor meant is that business and businesspeople tend to be excessively narrow in their experience and their assessment of situations and issues. There are polymaths in the Canadian business community, but they are rare.

The deadening influence of a trade-led foreign policy is made even more profound by the highly conservative and unadventurous nature of Canadian business. The general U.S. influence on Canadian life is magnified in the business world where a cheap Canadian dollar and ease of communications almost impose a north-south trade imperative. This traditional flow has been riveted in concrete by the North American Free Trade Agreement. There is now little incentive for Canadian businesspeople to explore wider horizons when all they need to fill their order books is a fax machine and copies of the Yellow Pages for major U.S. cities. This timidity has been abundantly evident in Asia in the past few years, and one now senses relief that the downturn in the economies of the Far East means Canadian business can justify not thinking about it anymore. The reality, of course, is that now is a time of tremendous opportunity in Asia for the brave and the confident.

There are cycles in Canadian journalism just as there are in public affairs. There are some signs that the country is now at the nadir of this period of self-imposed isolation. The voices railing against Ottawa's narrow and insubstantial foreign policy are getting louder and are barking from a number of different directions. Some fundamental reassessment cannot be far off.

One of the few advantages of enormous age and experience is that I have seen it all before. There was a time in the 1970s when the *Toronto Star* decided the age of credit cards and international flight made resident foreign correspondents unnecessary. They could sit in Toronto and rush off to events as they occurred. We are at a similar moment again. There are many problems with such a system. Foreign correspondents get restive easily. They while away the time fashioning office conspiracies. They dream up spurious reasons for travel, frittering away resources. Worst of all, they get out of touch with the daily movement of events and attitudes on their beats. They lose their analytical judgement of the countries they are assigned to cover. Their copy becomes unreliable. Soon someone has the bright idea it would make more sense to have the correspondents live abroad. This moment may be a particularly dark one in Canadian international journalism, but that only means the cycle is about to enter a brighter time.

JOCELYNE CÔTÉ-O'HARA

Jocelyne Côté-O'Hara is a senior executive, communicator and decision-maker specializing in strategy. Since 1986, she has led in the restructuring of the Canadian telecommunications industry in a competitive marketplace: first as vice president, government relations, of BC Tel; later as founding president and CEO of Stentor Telecom Policy Inc., the think tank and policy-development corporation of the Stentor Alliance, on behalf of Canada's regional telecommunication companies.

She is a member of several corporate and voluntary boards, including Manitoba Telecom Services Inc., Xerox Canada, the Federal Government Communication Research Centre, the Hot Docs documentary film festival, and Interlink, an association for cancer and nursing.

Previously Côté-O'Hara held increasingly senior positions with various federal and provincial government departments and was a senior staff member in the Prime Minister's Office.

She has served on several federal task forces and advisory councils dealing with public policy on women in the workforce, the digital economy, and trade policies and agreements. She chaired the Advisory Group on International Trade in Telecommunication and Computer Services throughout the NAFTA and GATT negotiations.

PAULINE COUTURE

Pauline Couture has established a solid reputation as a communications strategist and senior adviser to top executives in such sectors as broadcasting, telecommunications and financial services. She has served on a number of government task forces and advisory councils at the provincial and federal levels in the areas of economic development, social change and the impact of the information age.

Couture serves on the executive of the Board of Governors of the Canadian Journalism Foundation and is editor in chief of the foundation's upcoming Media and Society series of papers. She has been a director of the Toronto International Film Festival; a member of the executive committee of the Trillium Foundation, Canada's largest foundation; and was founding chair of the Caring Communities Award, a unique program to recognize innovation, dedication and commitment to exceptional action at the community level.

She is a former journalist, commentator and columnist with the *Ottawa Journal*, the Canadian Press, the CBC, Radio-Canada, CTV, TVA, *Your Money, Quebec Business* and the *Globe and Mail*.

How Journalism Struggles to Keep Technology in Its Place

IN THE EARLY 1970s, when one of us (Jocelyne) was a researcher in urban planning and the other (Pauline) was starting out in journalism, there was only one way to do a piece of investigative research: the hard way.

For example, checking out court proceedings or real-estate titles was like trying to buy fresh meat in the Soviet Union. You had to line up at a dusty counter somewhere in the bowels of a musty old building. You had to ask for one kind of piece of paper, then take it over to another place and wait in line again. If you didn't find what you were looking for the first time, you had to start over again.

Fact-finding was laborious and linear. We had tremendous respect for the great investigative journalists of those years—people such as William Marsden, Sheila Arnopoulos, Victor Malarek, Richard Cléroux and Michel Morin—but we also knew *we* didn't want to spend our lives on this kind of backbreaking work. It simply took too long to get results.

In 1972, when Pauline started working at the *Ottawa Journal* at the age of 18, the newspaper was still produced on letterpresses. Skilled compositors would actually compose the pages of the newspaper by fitting little lead letters into moulds, and they would do it upside down and backward, as well. These lead moulds were used to make curved plates that could be fitted onto the presses. The process was noisy, time-consuming and required the collaboration of several skilled individuals. The men—there simply weren't any women in the press plant—would receive corrected copy from the desk through a vacuum-tube system that would shoot the paper rolls from upstairs to the right spot in the bowels of the building with a satisfying, self-important *thwac.*

Putting out a newspaper, even for a medium-size city like Ottawa, entailed a combination of social, intellectual and industrial processes that employed hundreds of people. There were many opportunities for one of those people to catch a mistake or to add value in other ways.

Even a true technophile can look back on those times with some nostalgia. As today's desk editors lay out pages with desktop publishing software and send them directly to electronic presses, sometimes by satellite, there is no denying that something—call it craftsmanship—has been lost. David Crane, economics editor of the *Toronto Star,* particularly misses the quality dimension added by the extensive participation of copy editors who asked questions and gave reporters "higher-level feedback." Today, he says, the quality of editing has deteriorated as desk personnel have become more preoccupied with pagination and other technical issues. He likens this development in newspapers to the advent of automatic banking machines or self-service gas pumps.

Crane and many other journalists do appreciate the tremendous flexibility, mobility and access to research resources that new technologies provide for them. But at the same time, many recognize that newspapers have been very slow to use all the potential of the technologies available to them—for example, in the areas of graphic design and closer relationships with their readers.

Lawrence Surtees, telecommunications reporter for the *Globe and Mail*'s *Report on Business,* says today's journalists have not begun to grapple with the new storytelling possibilities of these technologies. The imperative to produce pyramidal newspaper stories, designed to make it easier to lop off the less-important details if they produced too much hot lead for the composed page, has disappeared. The habit of doing it this way has not. "We're still writing Gutenberg," says Surtees. "How we tell stories hasn't yet changed. But there's no more reason to stay linear."

When exploring how technology has changed, and will continue to change journalism, it is useful to consider a set of values associated with journalism at its best. By examining how technologies help or hinder the ability of journalists to live up to those values, we can evaluate their true impact on society.

The July 4–10, 1998, issue of the *Economist* commented: "There is nothing wrong with treating news as a product for sale; but you must treat it carefully, because it contains ingredients like trust and decency that spoil easily." Most journalists, when they start out, would probably agree with the last part of that statement. They believe they serve the public and democracy. It is easier to maintain this public-service ideal in an environment such as a well-funded big-city newspaper or an arm's-length public broadcaster with a mandate and money. It is harder to maintain it when money is tight or when the pressure to bend toward an owner's other agendas becomes too great.

At its best, this value ensures that the public receives the information it needs to make its own judgements about everything from democratic elections, to public health and education, to which movies are worth seeing. The editorial integrity of a newspaper or media outlet is often one of its selling points. Some media owners have wisely used it in this way, instituting codes of ethics while providing a kind of firewall between the commercial and editorial sides of the business. At the best of times, there is almost always tension between the people who sell advertising and the people who produce news content. And that's probably healthy.

In the worst-case scenario, "the public's right to know" can be used to justify all kinds of unscrupulous behaviour and invasions of privacy. Despite the media's lofty ideals, public opinion now consistently ranks journalists below people toward whom the media seem to feel morally superior. This is a significant sign that things are not as healthy as they could be. "About a generation of research on audiences now shows that people have become increasingly skeptical of journalists just as they have [become] of politicians," says Conrad Winn. A professor, author of three books on media behaviour, and a pollster, Winn portrays existing research as showing "increasing numbers of people wonder[ing] if journalists have hidden agendas and if the politicians they cover are telling the full truth."

In the worst-case scenario, "the public's right to know" can be used to justify all kinds of unscrupulous behaviour and invasions of privacy.

The stated values of good journalism would also include accuracy, fairness, balance and completeness over time, since it's almost impossible to cover all the angles every day, and stories often evolve quickly. Good magazines traditionally employ fact checkers who follow up on every quote and fact stated in a story to ensure accuracy. Good journalists value relevance to their readers or audiences, sound research and good storytelling.

Although journalists are often less than honest in dealing with the people who provide them with information ("of course, this is off the record"), most believe that it is important to protect sources. This is particularly true if people who come forward with controversial or "hot" information have reason to fear for their own welfare or safety as a result of talking to a journalist. While this level of difficulty is exceedingly rare in North America, in many countries, the lives of both source and journalist can be at stake when a difficult issue surfaces in the media.

Even when no lives are at stake, people who give journalists information often feel they are dealt with cavalierly. In 1995 an American federal judge, Richard Posner, found ABC not guilty of fraud in an undercover *PrimeTime Live* segment on the grounds that people should know better than to trust any journalist's promise. "They break their promise, as any person of normal sophistication would expect," the judge wrote. "If that is fraud, it is the kind against which potential victims can easily arm themselves by maintaining a minimum skepticism about journalistic goals and methods."

Somewhat surprisingly, under the circumstances, a recent Gallup Poll for the *American Journalism Review* finds that television newsmagazines are considered more credible and trustworthy than national newspapers such as the *New York Times.* The American public showed Gallup pollsters a healthy dose of mistrust, however, of information that comes from news on the Internet, half-hour entertainment news programs, and radio and television talk shows.

Most journalists believe they have to demystify: to help people understand complex issues that affect their lives. A corollary to this is that they often view themselves as gatekeepers to certain truths.

Journalists tend to have trouble with the idea of their role *within* society. They often view themselves as outsiders with the right, indeed the obligation, to watch and to comment. Discussions of their obligations are more difficult. By the nature of their work, journalists are highly resistant to rules. They recognize no one's right to regulate them or to certify who can or cannot be a journalist. For this reason, journalism is not a profession in the traditional sense of the word, but rather an intellectual craft.

Freedom of expression is something journalists tend to believe in, particularly for themselves. Some pride themselves on the number of times their stories have been "lawyered," particularly if the articles are then published or aired. Pushing the envelope is part of the thrill.

But the best journalists also recognize the limitations of the form. Deadlines every 24 hours, or even sooner, do not allow for much reflection when you are recording history on the fly. Journalists come to rely on networks of experts and opinion leaders whom they consult according to the subject matter. In this way, there is a subterranean influence that primary readers or consumers of journalism do not always see.

David Shenk, a U.S. journalist who wrote *Data Smog: Surviving the Information Glut,* says the barrage of data at the fingertips of all the participants in these discussions among politicians, lobbyists, columnists and journalists results in "a virtual anarchy of expertise" that can leave readers and viewers feeling they have stepped into a zero-gravity experiment.

New information technologies have an impact on all of these values and practices.

We think of watershed moments in any discussion of whether faster news is better news: the assassination of President Kennedy, when most North Americans first followed an event live on television; the Gulf War, when CNN truly made its mark; the death of Princess Diana, with its snowballing emotion that forced the Royal Family to change its style of operation; the October 1997 550-point drop in the Dow-Jones average, when a U.S. study showed that fully 11 percent of attentive news consumers switched to the Internet to follow the story as it unfolded there; and, finally, the White

House sex stories, starring Monica Lewinsky, first broken by Matt Drudge in his Internet gossip column and taken up by thousands of chat groups.

Information junkies who follow a spectrum of media know that not everyone has reacted in the same way. Network television newscasts still open with stentorian announcements of top breaking stories that they seem to believe are completely new to their audiences, even if all-news networks, radio and Internet sources have been following the story for hours. In August 1998, CBC Television carried a completely outdated documentary on Bill Clinton and Monica Lewinsky that was produced a few months earlier.

The Lewinsky story has revealed a strong dose of fear, loathing and paranoia in the traditional media. It has not been pretty. Terrified of being left behind, journalists with long, distinguished careers abandoned verification procedures and violated long-held taboos. Prime-time television news programs began to feature open discussions of bodily fluids and sex acts (unthinkable just a short while ago) and unverified speculation about presidential behaviour based on manipulative leaks from all sides. The more journalists sank into this morass, the more their status in public opinion sank—and the more the president's rose.

A dispassionate observer has to wonder whether journalists might be more in tune with their audiences if they made greater use of the new technologies' ability to listen to people. What the opinion polls, Internet chat groups and other forums were uncovering was a profound rejection of the role the media had designed for themselves. The public was saying, "We never appointed you to be the sex cops, or any other kind of cops, for that matter. In his shoes, I would lie, too. And what does it have to do with his ability to be a good president?"

It's unlikely the media would have been quite so vulnerable to public opinion if new technologies had not so dramatically increased the speed at which new information, reliable or not, comes to light.

If you do happen to need to trace a paper trail of real-estate transactions (for example, to prove that there is corruption or conflict of interest), the kind of access and speed that new technologies provide is virtually priceless. No longer do you have to stand in line or guess where something might be. Smart search engines organize the search for you and find possibilities in a matter of seconds. No one questions your credentials, and no one tells you what to think about it.

These new technologies transform the magnitude of the job you can do and radically reduce the time needed to do it, although deriving meaning from the data still requires a focused, disciplined approach and the intelligence to connect the dots.

In a recent example, the *Globe and Mail* took eight weeks of painstaking microfilm research to verify a claim by Justice Ian Binnie of the Supreme Court that he was quoting an article from that newspaper when he used the expression "faggoty dress-up party" in a speech. His use of the phrase had been deemed widely offensive. If the said party had occurred after 1977, when the *Globe* started up its electronic database, a simple word search would have found the reference immediately. As it happened, Justice Binnie was vindicated when a sharp-eyed *Globe* librarian found the reference in the January 13, 1967, edition of the paper.

The new ease and speed of research may well be the single greatest gift the technologies have brought to journalists. But, of course, many of the journalists' readers, viewers or listeners now have access to the same sources of information, with two consequences: they may not need the journalist to filter the information for them, and they are therefore more critical than they used to be. Who needs a gatekeeper if you have a key for yourself? Many journalists and media outlets are only beginning to grapple with this idea, although they *have* begun to understand that they are actually competing for people's time.

The Lewinsky story has revealed a strong dose of fear, loathing and paranoia in the traditional media.

In the on-line world, scarcity applies to attention, not information. Meanwhile, people are becoming more discerning about what they do with their precious time. The leisure society is far from being a reality for many people. Most people we know are working longer hours than ever. The free time they do have is shared among a number of different activities, and chances are they spend less of it than they did before reading a traditional newspaper or watching a traditional newscast. Certainly Nielsen data show overall television viewing is down in Canada by at least an hour a week compared to a decade ago.

This development creates mounting competitive pressure on all types of media, and consequently on journalists. Much of the source information they use is out there for anyone else to see. And while many people may be content to wait for information spoon-feeding, the highest-value readers and listeners —the ones with little free time who are most desirable to advertisers—are just as likely to be too impatient to wait.

For some time now, we haven't relied on newspapers when we want information on our stock portfolios. In an interim phase that lasted a couple of years, Pauline's husband paid $30 a month, then $15 a month, for a daily fax of his current portfolio prices at the end of the trading day. That generated some temporary revenue for the *Toronto Star,* but his new system of keeping the prices updated on his computer desktop is free—and far more satisfying. And it has reduced his involvement as a customer of the *Toronto Star,* which might have been smarter to make the service available at a lower cost or to ensure his loyalty through the transition to a Web- or e-mail-based solution.

At the *Toronto Star,* economics editor David Crane is mostly very happy with the advantages technology has brought to his work. He sees the greatest benefits in research and communicating while travelling. He gives the example of a meeting of the International Monetary Fund in Washington, where he can't possibly attend all the briefings. But he can catch up on them immediately afterward, since Reuters, AP and Dow-Jones cover them or post transcripts. In this way, he is able to give his Canadian readers a Canadian analysis of the big picture, something that simply wasn't possible before. No Canadian newspaper can afford more than one journalist on an important economic story abroad, but that journalist can use technology as his or her eyes and ears to cover a lot more ground.

Of course, only a small percentage of Canadians are actively participating in on-line chats and interactive forums, but this number will grow fast.

Similarly, when Crane travels, he feels no nostalgia for the days when reporters had to call in and say, "Gimme rewrite!" Or, worse still, rely on the vagaries of a remote telegraph office. Dictating a story painfully over long-distance lines to a clerk whose hearing and typing skills might not be perfect was never any fun. Now, even from Beijing, Crane can file his stories at his convenience 24 hours a day in minutes. He can also do extensive research from home or a hotel room anywhere. These are real gains in productivity and quality, but they're accessible to anyone with a computer and a modem. So the pressure on journalists to add value is suddenly increased.

Of course, only a small percentage of Canadians are actively participating in on-line chats and interactive forums, but this number will grow fast. Still, what is clear to anyone who follows a minimum of Internet activity, even passively, is that there is a formidable amount of self-expression going on. Some of it is hateful, excessive and ugly. Some of it is fascinating, original or funny. All of it is happening without the mediation of journalists.

In the 1980s, when companies began to go straight to electronic markets to raise money, bypassing the traditional bank loan, this phenomenon was known as "disintermediation." To some extent, journalists face the same loss of their powers as "middlemen" between events and the public.

From direct-coverage television (CPAC) to Web-based stock-market indicators, Internet chat rooms and e-mail newsletters, people are greatly diversifying their sources of information. However, it is interesting to note that while all this cacophony of expression is going on through highly specialized newsgroups (*alt.activism.age-restrictions* and *alt.adopt.latvian.babies* are real examples), the transmission speed of news and the fierce competition for people's time are leading to a polarization of trends. First, there is the explosion of global, specialized audiences that can now be viable because of instant communications. On the other end of the spectrum, though, is the predictable herd behaviour around high-profile news stories everyone wants to talk about.

Journalists who wish to maintain their public-service mission and add value that people cannot get otherwise are going to have to examine their own behaviour carefully in the future and decide whether to keep this merry-go-round spinning or get off.

Public opinion has already decided journalists are not delivering as much value as they used to. This is only going to get worse as people develop additional avenues for cross-checking what journalists tell them and form their own opinions about events.

Matt Drudge has already proven that he can respond quickly and effectively to criticism from the "mainstream" media. It has become more difficult to respond to him, especially since his early allegations in the Monica Lewinsky affair, originally judged scurrilous, have proven to be true.

Few journalists, as yet, are posting their e-mail addresses at the end of their pieces in print, on radio or on television. But those who do find the interchange with their readers brings a whole new dimension to their work. The *Toronto Star*, which is a large and powerful newspaper in Toronto, is difficult to find on newsstands in Ottawa and Montreal, let alone Winnipeg or Vancouver. But David Crane says he now has echoes of his work from readers around the world because his columns are now available on the *Star*'s Web site. This is one side of the coin.

The other side is a much more horizontal model of information exchange that people are experiencing in many other walks of life: business, medicine, politics, et cetera. Doctors, for example, are finding many more patients have researched the latest trends on their symptoms and illnesses on the Net and often have new information even they haven't had time to obtain. It changes the relation of "authority" to "layman." Journalists are bound to have the same experience as technologies spread and as the public achieves the next stage of media literacy.

As increasing amounts of information are available on-line, we will see more development of meta-data, or data about the data, that will make it more usable, more searchable and easier to analyze. We believe that as this happens it will be possible to gain a higher order of understanding of certain phenomena. When you assemble the results of many studies and articles in more usable ways, the learning that results will be more authoritative and more grounded in experience and reality—in theory.

What could happen instead, and journalists would be the first agents of contagion if it did, is that decisions based on meta-data could be terribly wrong, with far greater consequences precisely because they are based on higher-order information. Making mistakes in high gear takes you much farther.

So, as we have seen, new technologies open a can of worms because they create a situation in which information circulates ever faster.

Even articulating this problem is difficult. And yet thinking journalists must be among the first ranks of those facing this challenge. It will give them a way to reconnect with some of their primary values, such as public service and relevance.

So, as we have seen, new technologies open a can of worms because they create a situation in which information circulates ever faster. They also drive a whole series of problematic and egregious invasions of privacy.

We have seen that journalists can be all too delighted to rush into the breach, although many will profess disgust at some of the depths to which they and their colleagues have sunk. In Canada there has traditionally been little appetite for invading the privacy of public figures. Pauline remembers an evening the month after the first Quebec referendum in 1980, when two much older male journalists convinced her to accompany them to the hotel suite of a senior Canadian politician. They assured her they would find there a party in full swing, where hot background information on the constitutional talks could be gathered.

The party consisted of the politician, lots of champagne, a young bare-chested man who appeared to be about 16, and a large dog. Did any of us ever write anything remotely connected to this scene? No. What would happen in 1998? Who knows?

One thing is certain: in 1998 we have lived through the O. J. Simpson trial and the Monica Lewinsky saga. We have heard far more than we care to know about sexual activity, betrayals of friends and family, and other obscenities. And it's highly unlikely we would know about them on such a grand scale if there were not technologies and competition spewing information faster and faster.

In Jocelyne's political days, she saw media feeding frenzies on occasions such as meetings of the G7 group of countries, where journalists outnumbered all the delegates and officials. The media briefings actually became the meat of these events, shifting the focus away from the discussions of critically important issues. This power shift from the elected to the media rendered the sessions irrelevant in terms of substance and reduced them entirely to media events. G7 meetings are even less important today than they were in the mid-1980s.

Those who follow the events on the agenda of the G7 are developing many other ways to follow the economic and social issues they care about. Anyone who doubts this has only to examine the history of two recent initiatives that, respectively, succeeded and failed because of public opinion mobilized electronically.

In the first instance, the world gained a new treaty banning land mines through the mobilization of interest groups and politicians worldwide, largely supported by Internet communications. Similar tactics were behind the success of the group led by the Council of Canadians in Canada, with help from like-minded groups around the world, which put a stop to the Multilateral Agreement on Investments (MAI), for the moment. The lesson to the decision-makers in the latter case was to shift more of the talks behind closed doors. It remains to be seen whether that kind of strategy will effectively remove concerned citizens from the debate. We somehow doubt it.

In both examples, the media reported very little on the electronic citizens' initiatives, which helped these groups take the politicians by surprise. But broader knowledge of these kinds of grassroots movements would certainly be in the public interest.

Politicians who ignore the impact of information and communication technologies on important public-policy questions do so at their peril. In all likelihood, the media will become less important as the main vehicle for reaching the people, especially if they are again caught unawares, as they seemed to be on the MAI.

We are only beginning to experience the extensive fragmentation of the collection and dissemination of news with cable, satellite and Internet becoming viable and robust alternatives to the traditional print and broadcasting operations. The information highway analogies of the past decade included a proliferation of newspapers on-line—Gutenberg in the hands of the masses. The economics are not yet clear: there are many newsletters, journals, newsgroups and services on the Net, but few are profitable. There are a few exceptional success stories, such as the goods and services provided by companies like Cisco Systems, Amazon Books and Auto-by-Tel.

While journalists have the advantage of having grown up in one of the world's oldest knowledge professions or crafts, they must now operate in a world that is full of knowledge workers, brokers and managers. Now every institution and company wants and needs to be well established in the information age. And that means increasing their effectiveness through access to and mastery of information, data and technologies. In this environment, the media may need to live through the kind of cultural change that many other industries have undergone: for example, journalists may need to reexamine the knowledge-hoarding behaviour that characterizes a newsroom. Collaboration might be essential to meet readers' expectations in a timely manner.

The technologies now available to us allow anyone who can afford a computer and a telephone to tap into news from around the world, anytime. If our knowledge of human behaviour is any indication, most people will not do that nearly as much as they could.

Instead, they are just as likely to use the Internet to order a pizza from the corner or to find out the lineup for that night's hockey game. Over the past few years, the amount of foreign coverage in the traditional American and Canadian media has been dropping. The CBC and Southam have pulled back, closing foreign bureaus.

The emphasis on "news you can use" in all media has grown. From Martha Stewart to a plague of health-related stories, the media have increasingly talked to citizens as consumers. In some ways this is good. Empowering people to ask the right questions and demand high-quality services is a way of helping them control their lives. Eventually they may connect the quality of local health care with national and regional fiscal policies—or not.

Again, while some will take advantage of the opportunity to explore the world, others will be intimidated by the sheer volumes of information about events over which they have no control. They will seek to avoid pictures of starving Sudanese or to think about how to stop Saddam Hussein from taking over the Middle East.

The shrinking costs of an on-line presence will make intensely local information more viable and more attractive.

The old saying, "Build it and they will come," whether it's about a baseball diamond or a fibre-optic cable, encapsulates the way in which most technology has historically been brought to market. This is likely to change, if only because it is becoming too expensive as a business model—and too risky.

Journalists, however, have been caught in the flow of these developments in ways that are often neither in their own professional interests nor in the public interest. It is high time there was a more open discussion of these issues and a serious attempt to take back control of how and why technologies are used in support of journalism. Many readers and viewers are well ahead of the media in this area.

As technologies become more sophisticated and accessible, people are beginning to doubt the credibility of things they have long taken for granted. In the past, people suggesting that the 1969 moon landing was faked were treated as wing nuts. Today someone making those kinds of suggestions would give an audience far more pause because enhanced technological literacy helps people understand more readily how such a thing could be done.

The technologies now available to us allow anyone who can afford a computer and a telephone to tap into news from around the world, anytime.

"Programs such as PhotoShop may be the single best emblem of the immense new—eminently abusable—power conferred on humanity: With a little will and some patience, virtually anyone can do virtually anything to a photograph," says David Shenk in an article entitled "The Ethical Ramifications of Digitally Altered Photographs" in the October 20, 1997, edition of *HotWired.* And millions of teenagers are doing just that, going far beyond pasting moustaches on teachers they dislike or clipping a confrontational sibling out of a family portrait.

Journalists will have to develop codes of ethics and behaviour around new technologies that take into account a far more media-literate audience—and be prepared to explain them. The good news is that if they do that, it will greatly enhance their credibility.

While no one is suggesting that journalism is the place to win popularity contests, we feel that the current low regard in which the public holds journalists should be a cause of concern. We also feel that new technologies and the ones that are emerging are full of promise. Journalists should seize the opportunity to restate their core values in a new covenant with their audiences and to establish codes of ethics and methodologies appropriate to this new relationship. Everyone has a stake in their success.

STEPHEN WARD

Stephen Ward, associate professor at the Sing Tao School of Journalism, has 15 years of journalism experience as a foreign reporter, editor and newsroom manager. Prior to joining the school, Ward was the Canadian Press (CP) bureau chief in Vancouver and, from 1900 to 1994, CP's only staff reporter in Europe. Based in London, he covered major events such as the Gulf War, the Bosnian conflict, the troubles in Northern Ireland and the reunification of Germany.

Ward has a Ph.D. in philosophy from the University of Waterloo and was a research fellow at the Joan Shorenstein Center on the Press, Politics and Public Policy from January through June 1998. The centre, which is part of the Kennedy School of Government at Harvard University, will publish Ward's research paper, "Objectivity with a Human Face."

At Sing Tao, Ward teaches graduate courses on media ethics and issues. His research interests include the future of news objectivity, the education of journalists and the impact of the new media on daily journalism.

Pragmatic Objectivity and a New Ethic for Changing Times

At the heart of objective journalism is the idea that reporters should be restrained by truth, accuracy and fairness. People want straight news about their world, and objectivity, with its stress on factuality and impartiality, attempts to meet that demand. News objectivity is a means to accurate, relevant and unbiased information, which is essential for a democracy. But objectivity, both as an ideal and as a set of newsroom practices, has fallen upon hard times. Michael Schudson, in *Discovering the News: A Social History of American Newspapers,* has noted that "a simmering dissatisfaction" with the very idea of objectivity has grown in academia and the wider society since at least the middle of this century. Scholars claim that objectivity is impossible because all knowledge, even science and scientific fact, is theory-laden and not value-free. Outside academia, our post-modern culture is skeptical about anything so seemingly outdated as truth and objectivity.

Not surprisingly, this skepticism has rubbed off on journalism. Media critics claim that news objectivity is a deception because reporters are political actors whose biases distort their reports. These skeptics say objectivity is too much to expect from journalists who are under intense commercial pressure to sell the news and please their corporate bosses. Moreover, news objectivity is said to be an undesirable, "exhausted" ideal because it has its own biases that undermine democracy, reinforce established power and promote unfettered capitalism.

The dispute swirling around news objectivity is unhelpful to working journalists and journalism ethics. Much of the criticism by media scholars and think tanks is negative, unbalanced and distorted by political ideologies and agendas. Criticisms of news objectivity dismiss the good effects that objectivity has had on journalism. Critics develop sweeping, difficult-to-prove theories of political bias that ignore the daily pressures of the newsroom. More important, the criticism often fails to go beyond the identification of biases to constructive, realistic proposals for reform. No new ideal to replace objectivity has emerged to guide reporting. Surely, after so much deconstruction of objectivity, it is time to reconstruct this ideal. To reject news objectivity isn't enough, because no matter how many studies unmask the pretensions of the media, journalism will continue to need—and the public will continue to demand—objective, responsible journalism.

One reason the objectivity debate has been unfruitful is that issues are framed by incorrect assumptions about objective knowledge. All sides in the debate assume that objectivity is defined by neutral facts, absolute standards and the absence of perspective. The skeptic has little difficulty casting doubt on such strong assumptions, and therefore objectivity is too easily refuted and the real issues are missed.

My notion of pragmatic objectivity, if followed consistently, causes a shift in our traditional approach to objective journalism.

There is, however, a more useful way of looking at news objectivity, one in which the concept of objectivity is redefined by stripping away wrong assumptions and acknowledging legitimate criticisms. I call my position *pragmatic news objectivity,* which is not the narrow news objectivity that emerged at the turn of this century and is now on the wane. That traditional view requires news reports to stick to the facts and exclude all interpretation. In contrast, my pragmatic objectivity preserves the idea of testing reports, yet makes room for perspective, evaluation and interpretation. This reform makes news objectivity more relevant for the journalism of the new millennium.

My notion of pragmatic objectivity, if followed consistently, causes a shift in our traditional approach to objective journalism. I start with the premise that everything we claim to know—our beliefs, descriptions, theories and points of view—is an interpretation of some aspect of our world. All knowledge contains some element of conceptualization, theorizing and evaluation. Even our perceptions don't provide an unfiltered contact with reality but, rather, a knowledge of ordinary objects viewed through a filter of concepts, judgements and expectations. What we know, from science to philosophy, using a metaphor made famous by the Harvard philosopher W. V. Quine, is a "man-made fabric" of theories and mental constructions only partially hemmed in by facts. Any item of knowledge is an interpretation, or interpretive claim, that is part of a web of mutually supportive facts, values and theories—what we accept as fact depends upon our theories and values, and the theories and values we accept depend upon facts. This web cannot be separated into two completely different kinds of statement: factual statements as purely objective and evaluative statements as merely subjective. Rather, statements differ in degree, ranging from highly objective to highly subjective, according to the support they get from facts, theories and other beliefs.

My second major premise is that an interpretation is objective if it is well justified according to the best available standards. There are three types of standards: empirical standards that test a belief's agreement with facts, such as standards for careful observation, controlled experiments, statistical measurement and prediction; standards of coherence that evaluate how consistent an interpretation is with the rest of what we believe, such as standards of valid reasoning; and standards of rational debate that include a commitment to persuasion and tolerance over force and manipulation, to fair consideration of rival views and counter-evidence, and to question one's beliefs. In many cases, standards will conflict. For instance, new facts may challenge established theory, or a new theory may radically reinterpret the facts. Imprecise trade-offs between standards will be required—how many contrary facts do you need before you change the theory? Objectivity, then, is a weighted, practical judgement. It is the evaluation of a belief's justification by balancing standards endorsed by a community of competent inquirers.

The implications of adopting this view are as follows. First, objectivity is the rational justification of our beliefs according to the best methods and tests, not the search for some absolute Truth. Second, objectivity is the complex evaluation of a belief through the balancing of several standards. Third, the test for objectivity is fallible. What we consider to be objective beliefs and objective standards change and are modified by inquiry. Fourth, objective standards are relative to the perspective of a community. We determine what is a fact and what is objective from within this perspective. However, we are not locked into our perspectives, which should be open to challenge and change. There are no absolute standards, but that doesn't mean every claim is as good as every other. We can judge that some interpretations or claims are better than others, given some standards. Fifth, the correctness of standards is determined by their overall usefulness to achieving whatever theoretical or practical goals we have, from understanding the genetic code and predicting earthquakes to communicating information. Knowledge is not the product of a neutral spectator whose ideas mirror external objects. Knowledge is the product of an active, problem-solving agent whose beliefs are objective because they help him reach his goals.

Pragmatic objectivity is compatible with our interpretations, values and perspectives. This view contrasts with more traditional notions that regard objectivity as incompatible with interpretation and evaluation. For example, positivists believe that objectivity is opposed to interpretation because only factual statements are objective. In this view, objectivity is a conspicuous absence of interpretation in statements. However, in my pragmatic view, objectivity is the conspicuous presence of tests of our interpretations. Objectivity is part of our interpretive activities; it is the testing of our interpretations by standards. Both the standards and interpretations are part of our web of belief.

How might this pragmatic objectivity apply to journalism? News objectivity is a form of pragmatic objectivity. All forms of journalism, including news reports, are interpretations of observable events with at least some degree of conceptualization, theorizing and evaluation. There are no value-free or theory-free reports. Some degree of interpretation and evaluation haunts even our most basic attempts to report an event. For example, a report saying that the prime minister of Canada was "stung" by accusations and "struggled" to reply is an interpretation. Descriptions of a standoff between Natives and police as an "illegal act" or a "legitimate affirmation of Native rights" are interpretations. Assuming that all of journalism is interpretive, what distinguishes news reports from commentary is the degree of interpretation and the degree of objectivity. Instead of dividing journalism into objective news and subjective opinion, it is better to see journalism as a continuum. At one end of the continuum are stories about accidents, fires and crimes that stay close to the facts. In the middle are news reports about protests, government decisions and social issues that contain context, judgements, interpretations and assessments of the significance of events. At the other end are complex stories about civil wars, foreign lands and political intrigue where hard facts are in limited supply, interpretation is king and the objectivity of the story is more open to debate. Moving across this continuum, we encounter stories with increasing distance from the known facts, increasing amounts of interpretation and judgement, and decreasing degrees of objectivity.

For pragmatic news objectivity, then, a report is objective to the extent that it is justified according to the best available standards. What are the standards for journalism? They are the same standards that apply to all inquiry—empirical standards, standards of coherence and standards of rational debate, as discussed previously. Moreover, journalism has developed its own specific norms and rules of objective practice. These norms come in two types: norms of factuality and norms of impartiality. By factuality, I mean truthful and relevant reports. Truthfulness is the use of accurate facts, quotations and paraphrases; it relies upon official documentation and reliable sources. Relevance means that reports are complete, contain the most important facts and address the most important issues. Impartiality requires balanced and neutral reports about disputes and controversy. In addition, journalists have translated these norms into a wide range of detailed rules, such as requiring at least two independent sources on a breaking story.

Sometimes these standards can conflict. For instance, the media's duty to inform a community about a pedophile released from prison must be weighed against its duty to respect the privacy of individuals. Where conflict arises, journalistic norms will require imprecise trade-offs. To evaluate a report as objective is to weigh and balance several standards. These standards are relative to the perspective of the reporter, his profession and his community. News objectivity, therefore, is a fallible and difficult evaluation. For example, is the relevance of a story decided by journalists, by experts or by what the audience finds interesting? Must a balanced report include all possible views or only credible ones? Who decides which ones are credible?

Adopting this pragmatic view of news objectivity has several advantages. One advantage is that it shifts the debate away from irresolvable, abstract disputes about the theoretical possibility of objectivity to more concrete questions about the degree of objectivity of a specific report in a given context. In my view, the issue of objectivity is the practical question about whether a report is plausible, given our standards. The issue is *not* whether a reporter makes an interpretation or whether pure facts and absolute standards exist. We stop asking the arid metaphysical question about whether objective reports can "correspond with reality." Furthermore, I hold that the issue is not whether reporters make claims or assumptions, but how justified and appropriate those assumptions are in a given context.

Objectivity is not the only valuable tradition in journalism, nor is it an ethic that must be followed rigidly in all contexts.

Another advantage is that pragmatic objectivity, as a matter of degree, is a flexible ideal that can be applied to a wide range of journalism, from news reports to background features on an issue. It makes sense to ask about the degree of objectivity of an analysis or even an opinion column. In contrast, traditional news objectivity can't make sense of the idea of an objective opinion column because it assumes that only factual statements are objective and that evaluative judgements are only subjective opinion.

A third advantage of my view is that the broad question about whether journalists should be objective becomes a pragmatic question about the usefulness of objectivity to particular types of journalism. Objectivity is not the only valuable tradition in journalism, nor is it an ethic that must be followed rigidly in all contexts. Objectivity may be more or less appropriate for investigative reports, civic journalism or political satire. The restraint of objectivity—of factuality and impartiality—should be felt strongest in news reports because the goal of such activity is careful, accurate informing. However, this restraint can be loosened for other types of journalism.

Finally, pragmatic objectivity skirts the two great bogeymen of objectivity and Western culture—the relativist and skeptic. For too long, the desire for objectivity has been driven by the fear that our views will fall prey to the skeptic unless we "prove" what we know or that our views are merely relative unless we base them on absolute standards. The pragmatic attitude is to cheerfully acknowledge that humans cannot reach absolute knowledge, but we can muddle along with the most plausible beliefs and standards. Relativism and skepticism make not a whit of difference to actual inquiry or practice because we will continue to require some workable notion of better or worse claims and better or worse standards. All that objectivity requires is a limited skepticism about particular beliefs and practices. We think from within a historical era and culture, but we can avoid a narrow ethnocentric viewpoint by keeping our rules of objectivity open to reform. We can do no better.

I anticipate four likely questions about a pragmatic theory of news objectivity. The first question is: Does the theory unduly weaken the role of facts in reporting? My answer is no. Facts remain a vital, albeit limited, test of objectivity. This is not to denigrate facts in journalism. For example, investigative journalists seek hidden facts to expose corruption. However, in other cases there may be no agreement on the facts or there may be insufficient facts to establish a claim. Purported facts may be false, manipulated or twisted. Facts do not carry their meanings on their sleeves; they need context. In opinion polls, for instance, the difficulty of correctly understanding the results shows that facts need to be interpreted and balanced against other things we know. In addition, the many cognitive skills required in journalism, from questioning assumptions to identifying trends, undermine the traditional model of the objective journalist as a passive recorder of facts. In an age when social issues are increasingly difficult and spin doctors tinker with facts, journalism needs reporters who can hypothesize, question, reason and imagine alternatives.

The second question is: Does the theory destroy the notion of objective reporting by claiming that all reports involve some value judgement? Many people believe that all values are inherently subjective and incapable of objective evaluation. My reply is no. Values are not merely subjective preferences. It is not enough to say I prefer or value *X*. I need to argue that *X* is worthy of rational support by showing that my value judgement satisfies the best available rational standards to some degree. To support my judgement, I will need to cite facts, theories and other values, and to compare various means to the same end. We may be unable to resolve a disagreement over basic ethical values but, given some agreement on fundamentals, we can rationally assess value judgements and positions that include value judgements. For example, thoughtful positions on substantive issues such as global warming, the treatment of heroin addicts and the best economic policy are not just arbitrary, subjective expressions of feeling. They are positions tested by standards and built up by making links between facts, theories, goals and values.

Journalists must make two types of objective assessment of value judgements: an assessment of their own value judgements and of those of the people in their stories. This is a difficult business with room for honest disagreement, but there is no escaping it because values are built into our web of belief. Furthermore, objectivity cannot require the setting aside of all evaluations as "subjective" because objectivity is itself a value. The apparatus of objective tests is endured because objectivity helps to create informed, democratic citizens, and democracy is part of our moral ideal of human flourishing. Objectivity, therefore, is based on a shared moral point of view. In morally, and politically, divided societies such as Bosnia and Northern Ireland, it is uncertain what it means to cover events objectively.

But reporters can use specific, impartial ways to report on disputes, such as avoiding loaded terms like redneck.

The third question is whether pragmatic objectivity violates a cardinal feature of objectivity—the neutrality of journalists when reporting on disputes or controversial claims. My reply is that pragmatic objectivity involves a limited neutrality that can take different forms in different contexts, and that is enough for objectivity. There is no perfect neutrality, if neutrality means making no assumptions or evaluations. But reporters can use specific, impartial ways to report on disputes, such as avoiding loaded terms like *redneck*. This does not mean the reporter detaches himself from all values. Instead, neutral routines are means to larger values, such as the commitment to accurate information. Similarly the judge, peacekeeper and referee are all neutral because they use accepted neutral procedures to achieve their larger goals of justice, peace and a fair game.

There are two forms of limited journalistic neutrality—one strict, the other more liberal. The form of neutrality deemed appropriate depends on the story. Strict neutrality means the reporter does not take sides, makes no explicit judgements and avoids inferences. This careful, restrained approach is appropriate for news reports about sensitive legal cases and disputes involving contradictory evidence and damaging allegations. A more liberal neutrality allows the journalist to make some evaluations and explicit interpretations in his report, as long as such interpretations are grounded in fact, logic and other objective tests. This liberalized neutrality is based on the principle of not prejudging the case, just as judges don't prejudge the evidence. Liberalized neutrality is appropriate for reports about social and political issues where reports need some interpretation, context and assessment. It is also appropriate for interpretive and analytical pieces. For example, the overall approach of a news report on the Canada-United States dispute over West Coast salmon catches could be neutral, in the sense of avoiding prejudgement and not rushing to the defence of Canada. Yet such a report could include a historical perspective, an assessment of the environmental effects of fishing practices, and an evaluation of a group's political strategy. The report is objective to the degree that the evaluations and historical interpretations meet the best available standards.

The final question is: What is the relationship between pragmatic objectivity and more committed forms of journalism such as investigative reporting? Some journalists, disdainful of the traditional, detached form of news objectivity, believe reporters should push for reform and write from an explicit, attached point of view. My answer develops the earlier point about objectivity being only one of several journalistic traditions.

First, it is a mistake to portray objectivity and attachment as always incompatible: the cool, detached observer versus the passionate, attached reporter. This opposition is too stark. Both the objective reporter and the crusading reporter are committed to goals, although the goals differ. The objective reporter values accurate informing through objectively tested reports. The crusading reporter values reform and uses argument and advocacy to prompt action. I believe journalism needs objectivity *and* attachment. Objective news reports on major issues should be accompanied by analyses, investigative stories and background features. Many stories can combine the techniques of objective and nonobjective journalism. For example, reports may combine the storytelling techniques of feature journalism with the hard facts and solid sources of objective reporting.

Journalism's history offers many examples of blending objective and nonobjective reporting techniques, from the magazine muckrakers of the early 1900s to the post-Watergate investigative reporters. We need both the passion of attachment and the restraint of objectivity to work together to produce solid, engaging journalism. Objectivity controls our penchant to speculate and promote. Attachment—whether in the form of thought-provoking analysis or the exposure of corruption—lifts journalism above a superficial coverage of events.

Some critics may wonder why we should bother to save objectivity. We should because reporting today needs the restraining hand of journalistic objectivity. This need will increase as we move into the next century. We live in an age of 24-hour news channels, of infotainment, of nine-second sound bites and of celebrity journalism. We wade through a glut of information—and misinformation—on the Internet. Fierce competition in the news marketplace calls for speedy production of attention-grabbing stories. Global economic and technological forces are pushing journalists to do careless or unobjective reporting. We need a journalistic ethic that pushes against such forces by restraining sensational reporting, emphasizing facts and logic and encouraging reflection on our news values.

Uncertainty about objectivity can lead to confusion in newsroom practice and the erosion of standards. Reporters and editors need a clear idea of what objectivity is and why it is valuable. Reporting is moving away from the cooler, objective style of reporting to a more personal, lively, opinionated style. At the same time, movements like civic journalism encourage reporters to promote causes. Even the more traditional newsrooms of the *Globe and Mail* and the Canadian Press practise an objectivity that mixes facts with interpretation and context. A new, clearer notion of objectivity would help journalists make sense of this change and guide their practice.

More generally, our democracy continues to need objective reporters who care about responsible communication. Objectivity restrains those who think journalists should only advocate causes. It restrains those who would use journalism to injure enemies and to pursue their own ends. To give up on objectivity, or to devalue it, is to leave the public sphere even more vulnerable to manipulation than it is today. In a culture that lacks confidence in objectivity, demagogues prosper and the quality of public debate suffers.

PAUL SULLIVAN

Paul Sullivan is the western editor of the *Globe and Mail*, responsible for news coverage for the three Prairie provinces, British Columbia and the Arctic. He has been able to work with narrative storytelling and tellers under a variety of circumstances because his career in journalism stretches across the media spectrum.

Sullivan has been the managing editor of the *Vancouver Sun*; vice president, editorial for Telemedia, which publishes *Vancouver* magazine, *TV Guide* and *Canadian Living*; a senior news producer for CBC-TV's *The Journal*; and the host of *Early Edition*, the CBC morning radio show in Vancouver. As well, he was a daily columnist for the *Winnipeg Free Press* and the editor in chief of the *Winnipeg Sun*.

He has launched several magazines, including *Sympatico NetLife*, and was responsible for the development of *Vancouver Village*, *Vancouver* magazine's Web site. Sullivan is the course director for the Web workshop of the Simon Fraser Summer Publishing Workshops. He belongs to only one organization, the Planetary Society, and one day hopes to be the first storyteller to visit Mars.

Storytelling and the Journalist as Shaman

LONG BEFORE Peter Mansbridge or Matt Drudge, there was the guy with the antler hat. He was the first reporter, and the evening news was held around the fire, deep inside the cave, while the sabre-toothed tigers prowled around out there in the primeval dark.

The big story of the day was the mastodon hunt, and Antler Hat really poured it on. He described the chase leading up to the kill, shamelessly flattered the chief hunter and salted the report with superlatives—the biggest mastodon ever seen, with huge, sharp tusks and great big feet that could stomp you to death. He described the kill in colourful detail, jabbing the air with his spear, letting loose a bloodthirsty howl that made those in the front row leap back in terror and surprise.

Then, after everyone was hooked, he went into detail—allocation of the spoils and the forecast for tomorrow's hunt, finishing with a beseeching prayer to the Mastodon God.

And that was the *Ice Age Gazette.*

Everyone at the fireside agreed that a well-delivered hunt report ensured success the next time the hunters ventured forth. The rest of the tribe could participate from the sidelines, the leaders were justly celebrated and the hunters had a chance to relive the exercise and reflect on what went right and what they'd do better next time.

For his efforts, Antler Hat received a double portion of mastodon, served right after Big Hunter got his. He was a powerful magician, both feared and loved. Alas, when the hunt failed to go well or there happened to be a dearth of mastodons, Antler Hat took the fall. Blaming the messenger has antediluvian antecedents.

These days we're not so easily impressed by the magic of the media. The postmodem edition of Antler Hat, or Anchor Man, is still in the centre of the circle, and he is still handsomely rewarded, but rarely do we leap back in terror or surprise, even from *The Jerry Springer Show.*

Perhaps this is just as well. As we become increasingly jaded about information delivery, we hold our purveyors to lower standards. And while media criticism is a growth industry, media critics rarely behead the objects of their ire.

Still, journalists would do well to revere their ancestors and honour those times when the news was cast with an elemental power that held through scripture, epic poems and sagas, troubadours' songs, illuminated manuscripts, fantastic travelogues and bestiaries, fiery sermons, folk songs, Horace Greeley, Ernest Hemingway, Norman Mailer and Tom Wolfe. I am half inclined to cap the list with Stephen Spielberg, since *Schindler's List* has the qualities of a contemporary epic. But it, like so many of his films, springs from the annals of his childhood mind, *Life* magazine circa 1944. As harrowing as *Schindler's List* is, it only obliquely reflects on us in 1998 as we huddle around the fire and wait for the news.

To gain the reader's consent for this invasion, the storyteller must reach back into Antler Hat's bag of tricks and mix a brew that will entrance the reader and draw him ever closer to the message to be delivered.

To qualify for the Antler Hat, the journalist must be inclined, no less than James Joyce, to forge the consciousness of the nation on the smithy of his (or her) soul. And if not the nation, at least the news. Performance has always been and always will be a key element of information delivery, but what I'm talking about is not mere performance. The story must be worth telling, and the information itself is only half the battle. To be a story worth telling, it has to reach down into and touch the deep mind of its reader or its listener. It can descend all the way into the medulla oblongata, the lizard brain, arousing the primeval beasts of survival—lust and fear—but it must also, like Dante, come up again into the light of the cerebral cortex to reconcile the elemental with the reflective, or as we say at the *Globe and Mail*, give the story context.

To gain the reader's consent for this invasion, the storyteller must reach back into Antler Hat's bag of tricks and mix a brew that will entrance the reader and draw him ever closer to the message to be delivered. These techniques are familiar to anyone who has taken English 101: the story must have a beginning, middle and end. It must carry the reader along with rising action and suspense, driving to the climax, and then deliver the resolution, which may also look toward the future.

The people in the story are more than subjects—as the novel is populated with characters, so the people in a journalistic story characterize the message. And while Anchor Man is as enthralled as Antler Hat by the newsmakers, celebrities and Big Hunters of the day, there is a lovely quote from popular historian Will Durant about "real people," as you hear them called in the newsroom, that nicely sums up the kind of consciousness-forging stuff we're after:

> Civilization is a stream with banks. The stream is sometimes filled with blood from people killing, stealing, shouting and doing the things historians usually record; while on the banks, unnoticed, people build homes, make love, raise children, sing songs, write poetry and even whittle statues. The story of civilization is the story of what happened on the banks. Historians are pessimists because they ignore the banks of the river.

So far I've avoided assigning a label to this method or school of journalism. Rest assured, taxonomy junkies, that it comes with one. It's called narrative journalism, and they even hold conferences on it. Its patron saint is Tom Wolfe, although when he wrote *The Electric Kool-Aid Acid Test* and *The Right Stuff,* it was called the New Journalism. And as we, ahem, stand on the threshold of the New Millennium, it is important to note that we have passed the silver anniversary of "The Birth of the New Journalism: Eyewitness Report by Tom Wolfe," that seminal document of narrative journalism published by *New York* magazine in February 1972. The man who was to write the seminal novel of the 1980s, *The Bonfire of the Vanities,* boldly declared that the novel was dead, the action was in nonfiction, and reporters were adapting narrative techniques to their reports. Hunter S. Thompson and Norman Mailer would join Honoré de Balzac, T. S. Eliot and Charles Dickens in the Antler Hat Hall of Fame.

In a 1995 interview with Steve Hammer on the Internet, Wolfe regretted naming the New Journalism:

> Incidentally, all movements labeled as "new" are doomed. They die very quickly. What was new about it was the utilization of techniques in journalism that had previously been used only in fiction. Today, the techniques are very much known by writers for newspapers, and in magazine work. And they just go ahead and use them and you can pick up, let's say, *Rolling Stone*, or for that matter, almost any magazine that allows good writing in its pages, and you'll find examples of it. It's not just talked about anymore. Which I think is a good thing.

> I regretted in many ways publishing the book *The New Journalism* [the essay grew into an anthology with a Wolfe introduction in 1973], because in effect it set down a bunch of rules and standards by which non-fiction could be practiced. In a way that undercuts what made it fresh and original. There were no rules for non-fiction when the New Journalism began. There was a great deal of spontaneity and there was never the sense that it was something to live up to. That was the charm.

Hammer raises a note of caution about the man he calls the "Father of New Journalism." Of course, anyone who read Hemingway's war correspondence or listened to Edward Murrow understands that narrative journalism did not begin with *The Electric Kool-Aid Acid Test,* but Wolfe was among the first to expose the tricks to public view. Father Tom himself continues to send in fresh and original reporting, as evidenced in the 1996 *Forbes* article, "Sorry but Your Soul Just Died," which announces that sociobiology will presage the next great revolution in thought. The human psyche, mind, or soul is genetically hardwired, and we are all biologically predetermined. Free will is assigned to the trash heap of science, along with parthenogenesis and phrenology. Just as Friedrich Nietzsche reported that God is dead at the end of the 19th century, Wolfe declares that the soul is dead at the end of the 20th.

This tendency to declaim is a curiously effective element of narrative journalism. There is a rolling sonority that attends the rising action in a narrative journalistic piece. Even if the writer is writing about small things, and Wolfe never does, the remorseless suspense of the narrative driver leads the reader to believe he or she is witness to the unfolding of history. John McPhee, the former *New Yorker* writer revered by writers of interminably long magazine articles, has just written an exhaustive series on geology, which would sink into a quagmire of irrelevance if not for his surefooted command of the narrative. All that detail about tectonic plates and alluvial plains seems to be taking us somewhere very important—to the message, or in fictional terms, the climax and the resolution.

The Antler Hat Hall of Fame is not exclusively a male preserve—Oriana Fallaci and Joan Didion immediately come to mind—but to date, most of the hat gang has been comprised of men. This will change as the number of female journalists acquires critical mass, and the odds are that many more will feel the call of the ancient narrative magic.

Canada, with its reputation for self-deprecation, and its confused, unresolved national saga, may seem an unlikely progenitor of narrative nonfiction virtuosity, but there have been notable practitioners, some of whom I've witnessed in the act. Mark Starowicz, the man who created CBC's *The Journal* and *As It Happens,* is typical of the type. His consuming ambition to tell the world about the world matches his storytelling zest. In everything he does, in documentaries about Quebec or orangutans, he is unable to resist playing to the front row, fireside.

There are others I have encountered or observed: Allan Fotheringham, Ian

Brown, Barbara Amiel, Ric Dolphin, Daniel Wood, Michael Valpy, Farley Mowat, Terry Glavin—all of whom are right at home in the centre of the circle.

In fact, there are, as Tom Wolfe mentions, numerous newspaper and magazine writers who have adopted narrative techniques in their writing. For most of them, it's not something they picked up at journalism school or while paying their dues writing for the *Podunk Daily Planet,* but something that is, with apologies to Robertson Davies, bred in their bones, or maybe hardwired is a better way to put it.

In fact, there are, as Tom Wolfe mentions, numerous newspaper and magazine writers who have adopted narrative techniques in their writing.

Melanie Phillips, the co-inventor of a computer program called Dramatica, which helps writers plan out their stories and characters, says that "any good story is an analogy to the viewpoint of a single human mind trying to resolve an inequity." To her, narrative has a scientifically verifiable basis in nature—the mind is just naturally narrative: "To me, the mind is time—a standing wave in the brain caused by the interference pattern among different brain systems, operating on different time scales, that can change, learn, adapt and evolve."

If you don't buy the biomechanical model, how about the Judeo-Christian imperative, which works metaphorically, whether or not God is dead?

In February 1998, Boston University held a conference called "All Aboard the Narrative Train." Ron Rosenbaum, a pretty fair narrative journalist, explained the source of narrative journalism's power by resorting to John Milton. "'Justify the ways of God to Man,'" he quoted. "This, in a sense, is what storytellers do. This is what, at their grandest, perhaps most drunkenly aspirational narrative journalists try to do ... stories are often about man trying to control the uncontrollable."

At the conference, Tom Wolfe and his techniques were invoked over and over again and finally codified by chairman Mark Kramer in a kind of mission statement. Narrative journalism, he declared, "is an innovative journalism—narrated scene-by-scene by knowing, compelling authors who, after immersion in fieldwork, explore meaning by describing character and events, using personal, status-life details." If you can squint through the jargon, you can see Antler Hat at work.

No conference would be complete without the voice of Cassandra rattling the windows of the lecture hall. It will come as no surprise, therefore, that narrative journalism is threatened from all sides, struggling to survive as a species in the face of sound-bite news, shrinking "news holes," niche publication and the fragmentation of the audience, and on the Internet, the disturbing new inclination of the audience to take over the telling of the tale.

Whatever goes on out there in Analog Land is merely fodder for the myriad chat rooms of the Web, where people talk, and talk, and talk.

"Most of the writing in newspapers is dead," said one writer and editor. "You can't see the light, you can't smell anything and you don't know where you are."

"Newspapers were more interesting when they were filled with failed novelists and not communications majors," harrumphed another. "No aspects of this writing are new." The speaker, from Associated Press, admirably supported the thesis of this article by connecting narrative journalism to the age-old tradition of storytelling that he felt had been abandoned.

Finally Professor Kramer, unintentionally perhaps, echoed the thought of Melanie Phillips. "The intent of narrative journalism," he intoned, "is to convey the truth, not to express opinion.... *It's a time sculpture* [my italics]. You're creating a sequential, intellectual and emotional experience for readers."

Speaking of time, I can personally testify that journalists have been complaining for years, to anyone who will listen, that it's impossible to write great narrative journalism unless they get enough time and space. More money wouldn't hurt, either. In the January/February edition of the *Columbia Journal-*

ism Review, Steve Weinberg, a journalism professor at the University of Missouri, argues, however, that narrative journalists are convincing their editors that their method sells. "Sunday magazines are shrinking," he writes, "but this form of journalism is not. Newspapers are producing valuable, innovative, and sometimes beautiful examples of this against-the-grain kind of work. Writers are drawing readers into what are sometimes the equivalent of books, testing the notion that readers still like to read."

His prime example: "A Stage in Their Lives," a 16,000-word epic by writer Ken Fuson, published in June 1997 by the *Baltimore Sun.* Fuson spent four months with the cast of a high-school production of *West Side Story.* Weinberg liked it a lot. "On one level, his series is a tale about the production of a high school musical. On a deeper level it is a masterful story about teenagers coming of age in the complicated 1990s." To be an Antler Hat story, it must work at some deeper, even archetypal level.

Weinberg quotes Father Tom to support this notion of spending lavish amounts of time on the story in order to "stay with whomever you are writing about long enough for the scenes to take place before your own eyes." Scenes, not just facts, are necessary to the writing of compelling narratives.

Nevertheless, if you have to choose between storytelling and time, choose storytelling. Weinberg's piece is full of narrative heroes at work in the newsrooms of America, exhorting overworked reporters to inject storytelling into their quick-turnaround pieces.

Shortages of time and money aren't the only impediments to narrative journalism. Unless the writer has encountered narrative techniques in English composition or creative writing and has the wit to apply them to his or her work, it is unlikely they'll be taught at journalism school or passed down at the *Daily Planet.* Most writers are reduced to absorbing these tools by osmosis, which is not always the worst way. Still, it doesn't make any sense to reinvent the narrative wheel when there is a body of work accumulating, beginning with Wolfe's 1972 article/book and culminating in Pulitzer Prize–winning newspaper journalist Jon Franklin's *Writing for Story,* a book that has influenced many current narrative stylists.

The biggest threat to narrative storytelling, however, is the most intriguing.

Welcome to the World Wide Web. Millions of sources of information versus millions of information seekers, all interacting instantly (well, almost). People use the Web to find out quickly what's going on, but they're just as interested in adding their two cents just as quickly. It's as if there is no place but cyberspace, and it's only happening on the Web. Whatever goes on out there in Analog Land is merely fodder for the myriad chat rooms of the Web, where people talk, and talk, and talk. They are empowered to talk. They've got fabulous machines and equally fabulous software that give everyone the potential to be Antler Hat, after a fashion.

Regard Harry Knowles, postadolescent proprietor of *www.ain't-it-cool.news.com,* who has all of Hollywood waiting breathlessly to see what he and his fellow slackers think about the latest summer blockbuster. Harry has no storytelling skills to speak of; his only qualification is that he doesn't have a life. He's confined to his basement and acts as the Webmaster, the Head Spider in his sector of cyberspace, directing the equally uninformed opinions of the other bugs caught in the Net.

Harry and his fellow Web denizens are a new kind of people. They are impatient with storytelling. They are primed to interrupt, and they have the means at their command. The Internet has created a new fireside, where everyone tells the story, even if the closest they've come to the mastodon hunt is the chat room on America OnLine. At Web sites like *www.deconstruction.com*, everyone who inhabits cyberspace is empowered to tell the tale, and there is no one in the centre of the circle. There is just the circle.

On the Web, the conventions of the Tribe no longer apply. Nothing really happens. There are no challenges; there is only access. Time, a necessary plot device in Analog World, is real time—the omnipresent now. Narrative techniques are pointless—we're not going anywhere, because reality is mutating as we speak. It's virtual at best. No truth, no objectivity, no time.

There have been attempts to transfer narrative storytelling to the Web on sites such as *Slate* (*www.slate.com*), but if newspapers are an inadequate vessel for narrative storytelling, the Web is downright inhospitable—so many buttons, so little time. I defy the most single-minded linear reader to avoid being overwhelmed by the Urge to Surf. Even the literary *Slate* home page has hundreds of clickable options.

Of course, champions of narrative will remind us that, for the time being, at least, Death pulls the plug, and so the story ends. And it still begins. Resistance to narrative is futile. It is, after all, hardwired.

It is difficult to tell where the Web is taking us. It may turn out to be no greater a threat to storytelling than, say, the telephone, or narrative may die the death of a million bytes. Whatever else it is, the Web is a story that needs to be told, a job for Antler Hat, the Interlocutor of the Gods, the spinner of tales. To date, narrative storytelling has survived everything from the Dark Ages, to the Inquisition, to 1984. It is hard to believe it will succumb to the chat room.

For inspiration I return to Tom Wolfe, who back in the 1960s, the dawn of the era of future shock, proved that no modem tale defied the teller. In the *Forbes* piece, he continues to show that he is the inheritor of the Antler Hat. After a remorseless passage in which he surgically details the "attention-deficit disorder" fad and the absurd/tragic movement to subdue male schoolchildren with Ritalin, he is apparently simply overwhelmed: "America is a wonderful country! I mean it! No honest writer would challenge that statement! The human comedy never runs out of material! It never lets you down!"

It's as if Peter Mansbridge looked up from his teleprompter and started to laugh. It's a startling device that, in fact, breaks the narrative flow, but it comes at exactly the right moment when we are all leaning into the circle, beseeching Antler Hat for illumination. Wolfe restores the balance, allowing us to breathe and to express our building incredulity prompted by the above passage. It is the only point in the story that he breaks into what has become a patented device, and it is timed impeccably—a necessary catharsis.

It's a passage inspired by genius. The rest of us can only imitate clumsily or hold conferences or both. But Wolfe issues a challenge to all journalists, one so infrequently met in this era of sound bites and megabytes: Tell the truth, all of it, and make the people listen. It's as important today as it was in the cave.

NICHOLAS RUSSELL

In June 1998, Nicholas Russell took early retirement from his position as a professor in the School of Journalism and Communications at the University of Regina, where he had taught since 1983. Previous to that, he ran the journalism program at Langara College in Vancouver and was variously a reporter, copy editor, news editor, editorial writer and radio producer in a variety of media, ranging from the BBC World Service and Canadian Press to the *Whitehorse Star* and CFCF-TV in Montreal.

He holds a British Certificate of Journalism, a B.A. in English from McGill University, an M.A. in medieval English from the University of London, and a Ph.D. in journalism ethics from the University of Wales. His 1994 book, *Morals and the Media: Journalism Ethics in Canada,* has been adopted in most journalism schools in the country. Russell now lives in Victoria.

News Netiquette in the New Age

AT BEST, ETHICS IS AN INEXACT SCIENCE. Married to the ill-defined and amorphous field of journalism, it becomes "a swampland of philosophical speculation where eerie mists of judgment hang low over a boggy terrain," as U.S. academic John Merrill writes in *The Imperative of Freedom: A Philosophy of Journalistic Autonomy.*

In the early 1990s, it seemed—with the advent of a profusion of books, workshops and symposia on journalism ethics—as if the miasma might be clearing. And then along came the Internet.

The Net has raised a whole new subset of ethical dilemmas for reporters and editors, and many of the "old" ethical difficulties are simultaneously carried over into the new medium. In the beginning, Internet journalism was primarily driven by conventional news media converting their material to an on-line format in the hope that they could capture a slice of the market share and perhaps, in the long run, a piece of the rumoured riches. Although each new medium provides its own new challenges, the assumption—if ethics was even considered in the transition—was probably that the ethical guidelines subscribed to by conventional news media could be transferred in aggregate to the new medium. More recently, in addition, some entrepreneurs, convinced that there was a profit to be made, have initiated on-line news operations from scratch, without the benefit of an established newsroom behind them.

Journalists in the new media quickly learned that there were many unexpected pitfalls. For instance:

- Can editors ethically scoop up news features bought for newspapers from freelance writers, or should freelancers be paid extra for reuse in a new medium?
- Do reporters have to identify themselves as such when participating in newsgroup discussions and can those discussions be reported?

- Should reporters communicating with, say, "Dr. John Smith" on-line assume that's really the source's name and title, as they might with regular phone interviews, or should they be more distrustful?
- Should Internet news writers provide "hot buttons" to sites that are mentioned, even sites promoting sexism, racism, child pornography or other unsavoury, antisocial views?
- Should reporters scoop their own newspapers with stories appearing on the Internet hours or even days before they appear off the presses?
- Do readers of Internet news want different content than consumers of conventional news, and to what extent should this be served?
- With virtually unlimited storage capacity, should news sites make available to readers reporters' notes, raw data, interview transcripts or even "real audio" of entire interviews?
- How accessible should reporters and editors themselves be in terms of inviting electronic feedback and participating in debates on their reporting, editing or news choices?

These and many other issues will confront the responsible cybereporter of the future. Some of these problems—such as increased distrust of sources—smack more of good reporting techniques rather than of ethics. But it can easily be argued that good reporting *is* ethical reporting: Ethical journalists are those who act altruistically, putting society's good ahead of their own.

Broadly speaking, these new issues can be examined under two categories: problems of news gathering, and problems of presentation. Of course, many of the same ethical problems that are encountered in other media also emerge on the World Wide Web—issues of accuracy, fairness, privacy or conflict of interest, for instance. And even as specific media have specific ethical problems, so these also occur on the Web. Where weekly newspapers sometimes are tempted to become community boosters, so boosters of every hue appear on the Net. As radio stations must be constantly vigilant against being used as platforms for prejudice, so the Net seems to bring out the worst propagandists and hate-mongers. In this charged environment, journalists will face a multitude of new ethical dilemmas.

"Why?" has always been one of the journalist's "five W's," but it gains importance in reference to the Internet. The motivation of sources on the Net becomes vitally important. "Why is the source providing this material on the Web?" becomes as critical a question as "Who is the source?" and "What is being said?" A good example of this is the JonBenet Ramsey Web site (*www.rowanblewitt.com/ramsey*). Although this site was clearly created for the murdered child's parents by a public-relations firm, it was promoted as being "for the use of working members of the news media covering the Ramsey murder story, to allow them faster access to statements when they're issued than otherwise might be the case." But to what degree is material on the Internet fair game for reporters?

The Net, long prized by some precisely because of its anarchy, is truly "public" in the same way that an orator on an orange crate in a downtown park is public. And yet dialogue and debate on the Internet are conducted on "bulletin boards" or in "discussion groups." It is often quite simple to join. Many groups merely require a computer-to-computer message requesting membership. It is also easy to "lurk" on-line, monitoring conversations. So perhaps a better metaphor might be a public meeting.

The Net, long prized by some precisely because of its anarchy, is truly "public" in the same way that an orator on an orange crate in a downtown park is public.

Any member of the public can walk into a community hall and possibly even a Weight Watchers' meeting. But can reporters report such a meeting without first identifying themselves as journalists? If they walk in as citizens, they are, in effect, going undercover, and while sometimes necessary, this action should only be done with great caution. But once reporters have announced their presence, the event itself may be changed: participants may fall silent or speak more carefully or even leave.

Yet how many reporters would take the same precautions on the Internet? It is highly unlikely that journalists are going to interrupt discussions by announcing their presence and thus imply that everything thereafter is "on the record." And with many newsgroups, members can easily access earlier discussions, as they may all be archived, so suddenly the members have access to intimate debates—say, on sexual abuse—going back months or even years to the beginning of that particular discussion group.

Some newsgroups have already gotten into a lively debate about the permanence of the record. In print the newspaper reporter can publish a correction in a subsequent issue and hope that readers—and historians—will connect it with the original. But once the presses have rolled there is no way that reporter can expunge the original error from the newspaper's files.

Naturally most people don't want to see errors remain, but to what degree can we—should we—edit the words we have uttered? Net users can "flame" other users with vitriol one day, but should they be able to go back into that use-group's archive and eliminate the "flames," thus effectively preventing historians and journalists from ever seeing those messages, unless they were reading them as they were written? It seems likely that many Internet writers—when they recognize that what they say is "on the record" and visible to lurking reporters—may have second thoughts. Yet in established media it is very rare indeed for a reporter to give a source a chance to review the words uttered in interviews (or press releases or elsewhere) and to sanitize or polish them.

The sheer vastness of the Internet points out another problem inherent in the new medium: the difficulty journalists have to ascertain the provenance of their sources. Without impugning the work of ProfNet (*www.vyne.com/profnet/profinfo.html*), it is worth examining that particular resource as a case in point.

ProfNet describes itself as "an international cooperative of public information officers (PIOs) linked by Internet to provide journalists convenient access to expert sources." Most of those 2,100 PIOs (at 800 institutions in 17 countries) work with higher education, while some 20 percent represent "medical centers, national laboratories, non-profit organizations, corporations and government agencies." They have collaborated to provide a "Global Experts Database" on the World Wide Web. Researchers simply send messages to ProfNet, asking for contacts on their topics, and PIOs with potential experts on hand quickly reply with contact details. The effort is commendable and gives reporters access to all sorts of resource people they might not otherwise have discovered.

But who says these sources are experts in their advertised fields? Are they the best sources, or simply the most available. How do we know if they're merely the ones with time to talk to the press, or who seek, say, funding for their research? It may all just be a little too easy. And journalistic skepticism may have to be further increased following the purchase of ProfNet Inc. by PR Newswire, a public-relations agency.

If uncertain sources are a dilemma for journalists, hoaxes pose a threat to their credibility. A steady stream of would-be hoaxers seems to be out there ready to trick the media, to satisfy their own vanity or just to win a tavern bet. But early indications suggest that the Internet may attract more of these characters and provide the cover and opportunity for even greater deception.

"There is something incredibly seductive about information that shows up on a computer screen," wrote *Boston Globe* reporter David Armstrong in the September/October 1995 issue of the *Columbia Journalism Review.* "As a lot of journalists discovered after the Oklahoma City bombing," he added, "it can make gullible neophytes out of people who should be professional skeptics." Armstrong tracked two inflammatory messages that appeared on the Internet, implying there was a militia conspiracy at work. The messages were pranks, but dozens of reputable newspapers carried straight news reports.

Apart from problems of vulnerability, attribution, and veracity, the Internet also poses new concerns about privacy. In the United States, and somewhat less so in Canada, freedom-of-information legislation has resulted in the release of a flood of material for the media. But how will such open-government rules affect the Internet in any given jurisdiction? Many governments have already used the Net to distribute material such as full texts of documents and even Hansard transcripts of parliamentary proceedings. But will the desire to release official documents—such as cabinet minutes or senatorial memoranda—extend to electronic communication?

Should interaction such as private e-mail—even between elected officials—be regarded as private, or is journalism moving another step toward stripping public persons completely naked?

In 1996, citing the Colorado Open Records Act, a student newspaper reporter at Metropolitan State University of Denver wrote to several high-ranking state politicians requesting their electronic messages for the first half of January of that year. Such initiative is certainly good journalistic enterprise, but is it *useful?* Will there be a point at which requests for material merely inhibit the political process? It is possible that demands by U.S. reporters for open meetings have driven the "real" business underground so that "public" meetings merely become carefully rehearsed nonevents for official rubber-stamping of decisions already made in private homes or offices.

Should interaction such as private e-mail—even between elected officials—

be regarded as private, or is journalism moving another step toward stripping public persons completely naked? Particularly since Gary Hart withdrew from the presidential race in 1988, there has been an increasing fear that the impertinent stare of media scrutiny may deter competent people from running for office. The knowledge that even their most private electronic communications may be examined as far back as the archives allow might prompt many would-be political candidates to think twice about entering the field. (Which of us has never sent an e-mail that might look a little foolish if subsequently published on the local front page?)

As there may be ripe territory for journalists to seek politicians' e-mail, so some officials may be tempted to demand similar material from journalists. How will the media respond to a police request for copies of electronic messages from, say, the Unabomber? Or for demands for actual e-mail addresses of correspondents?

Of course, why should such pressures be treated any different than they have been in the past when authorities have demanded newsroom correspondence, reporters' notes, phone records or video "outs"? Journalists must always remember that if they ally themselves with law-enforcement authorities too readily, they will quickly be seen as being "bought," as being part of the system, and will no longer be considered trustworthy or able to criticize the authorities.

In January 1996, America OnLine (AOL) surrendered e-mail records to police who were investigating a New Jersey murder. The murderer and his victim had apparently met in an on-line "men-meet-men" group. Platform providers, such as AOL, may be different from regular newsrooms, insofar as they do not have the age-old loyalty to the U.S. First Amendment. In the murder case, an AOL spokesperson was quoted as saying that the company immediately complied with the search warrant.

Journalists would normally give considerably more thought on how to respond, worrying about the privacy of the people involved and about the public's perception. In the AOL incident, the public may have been best served by cooperating, providing the police net wasn't too wide (i.e., requesting addresses of everyone using the discussion group). But journalists must always ask if the case can be investigated by other means first rather than compromise their own integrity.

Quandaries about news gathering in the context of the Internet are undoubtedly vexing, but what about the distribution and presentation of that news once it has been acquired? Is there an ethical component to the problem of publishing material on the Net before it appears in a newspaper?

Perhaps the issue is merely one of the implicit contract between journalists and their readers, who expect to get their news as soon as it's available, and are probably unaware that a "blockbuster" story has been held to coincide with a ratings sweep, or that a newsroom has devoted additional resources to a project so that it can be entered in one of the various media awards, or that the exigencies of space, always a commodity in short supply, have delayed a piece.

Nevertheless, the nature of Internet journalism requires instantaneous release. Will journalists in standard newsrooms who are saving a story for a particular moment (i.e., to run on Saturday to reach the biggest audience) find themselves in conflict with their colleagues producing the Internet "paper" when they insist on immediate release?

It has also been suggested that some on-line journalists may be deliberately "scooping" their own print newsrooms in order to maximize the dramatic effect of their stories and create coverage by other media. In early March 1997, the *Dallas Morning News'* Web site published a report (before the newspaper appeared) of allegations that the TWA airliner explosion over Long Island was a conspiracy, thus provoking a furious debate on the Net.

Actually, in many ways, journalism is about leaving things out. Every moment reporters and editors are making decisions regarding content and display of stories. Indeed, in 1996 John Harder, news editor of the *Kitchener-Waterloo Record,* estimated that roughly 90 percent of the wire copy coming into his newsroom had to be left out for reasons of space. Michael Hallinen of *USA Today Online* has noted that "having spent years as a wire editor on a mid-sized daily, I know that you put in print maybe 5 percent of everything that flows across your screen." Such numbers are far from scientific, however, they demonstrate what everybody knows—that traditional newsrooms do not, despite the *New York Times'* motto, print "All the news that's fit to print."

Internet journalists quickly learned, though, that they could print "all the news." Every nuance of a story could be explored. Every source could be credited. Every press release could be available in full. Even—to extend the possibilities—every interview, as well as reporters' notes and tapes, could be transcribed verbatim or made available in RealAudio.

Some journalists may well be troubled by such concepts. Occasional legal cases have already indicated that reporters should eschew writing personal remarks in their notebooks (or drawing caricatures or passing derogatory notes around the press table) about sources if there is the faintest likelihood that these will end up as evidence in a courtroom. Perhaps—if notes are to be routinely exposed on the Net—even greater care must be taken.

But why should reporters release their most private material, which might include preliminary assessments of situations or of sources, to the denizens of the Internet? Some members of the public may reverse the question: "What have you got to hide? Aren't you in the information business, not the secrets business?" These notions suggest a new relationship with readers: an evolution of the editing function into a gathering function.

The preceding question leads to the whole issue of giving news consumers what they want rather than simply what they ought to have. One of the appeals of the Internet is the vast array of material available. It's somewhat akin to the small-town library user suddenly being given a user card in the National

Library or the Library of Congress. Net users can select the information they want, so there may be some resentment of editors who make those choices for them.

It is probably too early to ascertain whether the tastes of on-line news consumers will be significantly different, as both readers and content are still evolving. In December 1995 in the Canadian Daily Newspaper Association's *Newsletter*, Don MacLachlan, a Pacific Press director of communications, described a "totally informal, strictly amateur mini-survey" of some B.C. newsgroup users. When asked what they would like to see in e-papers, they responded in order of priority: classified ads (by a huge margin); archives; entertainment and leisure listings, reviews, etc.; and news, weather and sports. If such surveys are conducted widely, they will throw some fascinating light on readership—and may strike editors with fear!

One thing does seem clear: readers are going to want more than just the regular newspaper shovelled on-line.

One thing does seem clear: readers are going to want more than just the regular newspaper shovelled on-line. Some journalism schools are now teaching on-line news writing as a distinct, new style. Even if the material is the same, there will need to be some form of "value added" that has yet to be clearly defined. One Internet writer, Bob Wyman, has even wondered if, because of the predicted increase in local news, the on-line edition will ultimately become the dominant partner: "Could this get us to a point in a few years where working on the paper is seen as a purely technical job of squeezing content into columns while the on-line group is where all the 'real' journalism happens?"

Censorship is always a hot topic when it comes to the Internet. Is cyberspace American or Canadian? Whose rules apply? In a Canadian newspaper, obviously, Canadian "rules" of censorship apply. In other words, journalists respect the laws and values of their communities, expecting some official censorship during times of war, imposing some "self-censorship" in covering a few, difficult subjects, and exercising self-control with regard to the general standards that viewers, listeners and readers can be expected to tolerate. But with a world audience, whose rules should be respected?

The Internet has been developed largely by U.S. users, which has meant a strong lobby from First Amendment devotees who generally bridle at *any* limitations on content. Meanwhile other cultures—Muslim, Hindu, totalitarian or Marxist—may emphasize other values. Who is right? Is one system more valid than another? Or—as some Americans seem to wish—must the whole world accept the Net on U.S. terms? Inevitably that will lead to clashes, as has already occurred with the celebrated CompuServe/German contretemps. In that incident, Bavarian authorities threatened to impose German values by prosecuting CompuServe for bringing child pornography into their country. This move was greeted with howls of indignation by mainly American netizens, and every effort was made to circumvent the rules—not in the name of kiddie porn, but in the name of free speech.

Unfortunately two early U.S. court cases appear to suggest that taking responsibility for content also means taking legal responsibility. In a different incident, CompuServe was sued in New York for defamatory comments made on a bulletin board by a third party. The company won by arguing that—like a telephone company or a book dealer—it was merely a common carrier and not responsible for the messages therein. The judge agreed that CompuServe did not edit the material and therefore could not be held responsible for the content.

In a case against Prodigy, also in New York, the platform company lost precisely because it did take responsibility for its content: "A publisher has a responsibility to its readers to exercise editorial discretion," a Prodigy spokesperson was quoted as saying.

The option of choosing whether one's operation is more like a newspaper or more like a telephone company will likely not be available to most news Web sites. Since the majority have been developed by conventional news media using conventional journalists employing conventional news values, so they must be seen as—should be proud to be seen as—editors who take responsibility for their content. But difficulties may occur when such ventures provide wide-open letters to the editor or even chat rooms.

In those cases, to protect themselves and uphold the credibility of the news operation, a degree of editorial responsibility will need to be taken. Unpalatable as it may be to some, Internet editors will have to edit! Meanwhile ersatz publishers may start "news" Web sites without knowing anything about conventional media ethics. And clearly some citizens are determined to try to control content on the Internet; witness the attempts under Canadian human rights legislation to prosecute Holocaust denier Ernst Zundel for content of the U.S.-based Zundelsite.

Journalists and editors should, actually must, retain control of the editorial function, but is that a rearguard action on the Web? With traditional media—since the typesetter and proofreader have largely disappeared into obsolescence—the writer/editor is the last gatekeeper in the flow of news before the story reaches the news consumer. The radio reporter writes and voices the story; the listener hears it. The newspaper editor edits copy and lays out the page, it is printed, and the reader reads it. But the Web has the potential to change all that. The writers still write and the editors still edit and transmit the story out into cyberspace, but now a new gatekeeper may be inserted—the Internet service provider (ISP).

By and large, ISPs probably don't want the responsibility of monitoring content. But some consumers are demanding that the carriers prevent their children from accessing undesirable material. In response, software has been developed to filter material based on vocabulary, instantly blocking access to sites that contain certain red-flag words such as *sex, breast* or *abortion.* But obviously such words may well appear legitimately in news stories. Users can program their filters to permit certain exceptions, but whether they will bother, or how such a list would be developed, remains very much terra incognita. What is clear, however, is that another layer of external control on content is now possible, further eroding editorial responsibility.

There has also been debate about news links to antisocial sites—racist, sexist or otherwise.

There has also been debate about news links to antisocial sites—racist, sexist or otherwise. The freedom to point to other sites is seen by some as a basic freedom of speech. To paraphrase the sentiments of John Milton in *Areopagitica,* people can make intelligent choices, and the good will triumph. Critics, including this writer, respond that the news media must take responsibility for their actions and that facilitating access to, say, extreme pornography, anti-Semitism or bomb-making recipes is to contribute to the perversion of the young and the decay of society.

It's an uncomfortable call, since such material can already be found on the street or in the library, but it hinges on media responsibility: journalists must recognize that their work has impact on their audiences. If journalists believe they are merely pipelines and not at all accountable for the messages they convey, then they see themselves as neutered, mute witnesses to history. But if they admit that their work has impact on the audience and they want to participate in their communities and build a better world, then they must take responsibility for the consequences.

Thus, giving easy access to antisocial Web sites by providing links in news stories ("For more about bestiality, click here") may damage journalistic credibility, although it may be seductive. For instance, Steve Outing, an on-line guru and the operator of *Planetary News* and a very popular on-line editors' discussion group (*online-news@marketplace.com*), said in 1995 that "It appears to me that editors are more comfortable presenting controversial material to their readers on-line than in print, since merely providing a pointer or link is 'safer' than actually printing it." Outing was discussing the so-called "Unabomber Manifesto," published by the *New York Times* and the *Washington Post*.

Where is the line to be drawn? Thoughtful, collegial consultation and leadership are needed to develop a newsroom comfort level. Editors might first develop a simple guideline: "No links will be provided to sites that appear to advocate destructive activities. When in doubt, consult the senior editor."

A related issue arises with links to advertisements. If a news story describes a Ford recall or a Bre-X stock slump, should it contain links to Web sites promoting these products? Discreet references to sites that are mentioned in news stories are possible. For instance, the *New York Times* has used the following disclaimer with one of its Web stories: "Related Sites. Following are links to the external Web sites that complement this column. These sites are not part of the *New York Times* on the Web, and the *Times* has no control over their content or availability."

Why should anyone make such connections, though? Conventional news has never included such pointers (i.e., "See the Ford advertisement on page 17"), so it seems to be an unnecessary gesture that would be very much appreciated by the advertisers but which really provides little service to the news consumers. If product promoters are pressing journalists for this service, that's a sure sign that journalists should demur!

However, as ads are a fact of newspaper life, so they are a reality on Internet news sites. In newspapers, editors and advertising people generally collaborate to ensure that awkward conjunctions don't occur (the plane crash story beside an Air Canada advertisement, for instance). On the Internet, however, ads are typically inserted automatically—by the computer rather than by a sensitive editor/salesperson. Moreover, each ad is usually associated with a specific story. Incidents have already occurred, and they may be even more embarrassing before a solution is found.

Ads disguised as news present yet another issue. While mainstream media have mostly drawn a line in the sand, insisting on some identification of ads that resemble news, similar definitions have yet to be developed for Web journalism. The issue was hotly debated on the Web in June 1998 after an Internet manager gave a speech apparently calling for more blurring of the lines between editorial and advertising.

In the end, though, good journalism is good journalism, whatever the medium. After America OnLine played its elaborate "life on Jupiter" hoax (April 1, 1996), an AOL editor came up with a sobering conclusion: "I think that the lessons for online news are clear—at a time when anyone can be a publisher with a worldwide audience, standards for journalistic integrity and responsibility must be substantial and clear."

The issue is further complicated, however, by the necessity of redefining some basic premises. The role of the editor as filter may shift slightly, and the definition of news may be modified. Doubtless the waters will also be muddied by economic pressures, and there will be a real danger of greed overwhelming ethics. Katherine Fulton, in "A Tour of Our Uncertain Future," published in the *Columbia Journalism Review,* provides this thoughtful summing-up:

> I worry that the profits that now support the great journalism a democracy needs will disappear into niche businesses run by people with little interest in journalism but more imagination or staying power. I worry that too many of the best journalists will cling to the past, which will work about as well as it did for the guilds in the Industrial Revolution. And I worry that the most successful innovators—the ones who will write the rules for the new medium—will be technophiles who don't give a damn about the difference between a news story and an ad and who think the First Amendment is a license to print money.

On-line journalists will have to maintain the same level of integrity and self-confidence that off-line journalists do. As with all the earlier media of communication, there will be no fixed rules, no code of ethics, pinned on the walls of cyberspace. And, as every situation differs, so every cybereporter must have an understanding of how to make ethical decisions in tandem with the visceral will to produce fine journalism.

JOSH FREED

Josh Freed is an award-winning filmmaker, author and journalist who has worked in every medium except hammer and chisel. He currently directs, writes and script-edits TV documentaries and has a weekly page 2 column in the *Montreal Gazette*.

Freed started out in print at the *Montreal Star*, where he won a National Newspaper Award for best Canadian feature writer. He spent a year in radio at the CBC's *Sunday Morning*, then five years as an on-camera journalist at the CBC's *The Journal*.

Since 1990, Freed has directed and written many hour-long international TV documentaries for the CBC, BBC, PBS and A&E. His subjects range from the secret politics of the Academy Awards (*The Envelope, Please*) to a race to the North Pole (*North to Nowhere*).

Freed has written four bestselling books; won two National Newspaper Awards, including best columnist of 1997; and was awarded the 1995 Stephen Leacock Medal for humour. His films have won several Gemini Awards, and in 1996, his film *Merchandising Murder* won the World Medal for investigative reporting at the New York International TV Festival.

The Write Stuff

WARNING: THIS ESSAY CONTAINS SARCASM, HYPERBOLE AND OTHER CHEAP LITERARY DEVICES. THE READER ACCEPTS THESE RISKS AND THE DANGER OF IRRITATION AND OFFENCE THEREIN. 100% NO CHOLESTEROL.

THERE ARE TWO REASONS for the above paragraph. First, it's true and you might as well know it. Two, it's a way of getting you to start this essay by letting you know it could be fun. I'm a great believer in entertaining readers, and viewers, at the same time as you try to enlighten them. I think a strong opening, lively imagery, humour and good writing are critical elements of good journalism, whatever medium you work in, because they encourage the reader to read or watch your story. And most journalism is aimed at an audience, not at posterity.

Much as we'd like to think the reader has an obligation to read our story given the time, thought and serious research we put into it, "serious" doesn't count for much these days. In fact, it counts for less and less as people have more choice over what they read and watch.

Journalism is changing, partly because our attention span is changing, as a generation brought up on video clips and TV clickers has a shorter tolerance for being bored. And soon we will probably think this generation had a long attention span.

Click. Maybe you've already changed essays.

Print journalism is changing, too, using shorter, often breezier stories—so breezy you can get a draft reading the newspaper. As the *Economist* recently observed: "News is moving away from ... politics towards human-interest stories; away from issues to people.... Newspapers that used to be full of politics and sports are thick with stars and sports."

But you don't necessarily have to dumb-down your stories to liven them up. For me, the best stories combine style *and* content—giving the reader something to reflect on in a way that's enjoyable to read. I think what's often forgotten in teaching the five W's is that they can be helped out with a sixth. Along with who, what, where, when and why, it's nice to say, "Wow! This is a great read!"

I've spent my career moving back and forth from print and radio to TV and one-hour documentaries. I've worked in every medium except hammer and chisel, and I spend as much time worrying about how my stories are written as about what's in them. I like to think that when people start reading or watching my stuff they won't stop until they get to the end. I try to hook 'em and hold 'em and say something along the way. And while every medium has its own specific demands, good writing is critical to all of them—the backbone to any good story.

I think of it as the write stuff.

When you've got a great story or something original to say, you can coast on your content. If you're about to explain how the minister of education stuffed $500,000 in cash from a children's charity into his wife's purse, no one will care much about how you write the story. But if you're writing about the findings of the interim report of the Royal Commission into Whether or Not to Eliminate Interim Reports, you'd better find a way to liven up your story. For example: by writing your story as if it were an interim report.

How do you take an old subject and reinvent it, turning the story in your mind like a Rubik's cube to see if you can find a fresh approach?

Somerset Maugham once said that "there are three rules for good writing, but unfortunately nobody knows them." Most writers know there's no formula for How to Become a Great Writer—only infomercials promise you that, along with how to grow hair by singing opera to it. But there are some simple techniques that can liven up any story, and I'll touch on a few that matter to me.

Finding a Good Angle: Half of every story is the spin you give it, a fresh angle that makes you see an old subject in a new and interesting way. If you've got a good subject, or a good angle, the writing and telling is always easier. That's why the trend in Hollywood these days is toward "high-concept" stories.

I've written a newspaper column for the past decade, and the toughest part is always finding an idea. Or at least choosing one. In the words of 1950s New York columnist Max Lerner: "The hard thing is not to think up a topic, but to pick one out of the many that thrust themselves at you each day, out of the reading of wire copy and papers, out of books, travel, dreams ... and the ordinary contacts of an ordinary day."

Part of it is to sense the zeitgeist, the spirit of the moment: what are people feeling—are they mad, sad or glad? Are they in the mood for politics, or just a light summer read? What would you want to read if you picked up the newspaper?

Even if you're writing about one of the usual Canadian suspects—like cod wars in the Maritimes, dairy subsidies in Ontario, wheat prices in the West or Quebec's neverendum referendum—is there anything you can possibly do to make it seem new?

How do you take an old subject and reinvent it, turning the story in your mind like a Rubik's cube to see if you can find a fresh approach? How can you turn the story upside down and see it in a fresh way, then turn it upside down again? Take popular American columnist Calvin Trillin, in a piece from his book *Too Soon to Tell,* on the multiplying and often confusing number of new telephone area codes, a subject that should be dull. But Trillin comes up with a fresh idea: he wonders how the new area codes are chosen, then postulates that all the decisions are made by a single telephone bureaucrat, whom he calls the "Far Away Man."

> The Far Away Man likes area codes that are numerically close but geographically far away. I have always thought, for instance, that 718, which is now the area code for Queen's and Staten Island, was chosen for its numerical proximity to 818, the area code for the San Fernando Valley.
>
> A one-digit difference of 3,000 miles is just the sort of spread that the Far Away Man likes. He figures that a bad hangover or simple carelessness is often good for a one-digit dialing error. He likes the idea of someone in the New Jersey suburbs picking up the phone first thing Sunday morning to make his weekly call to his dear old mother back in Brooklyn and finding himself in conversation with a young woman who lives in Canoga Park, California, and is not terribly happy about being awakened at 6 a.m. by a strange man who insists on telling her how much he misses her lasagna.

Here in Quebec, where I live, we journalists are forever trying to come up with a new take on the same old political battles that never draw blood but never draw to an end. Recently I wanted to do a column skewering Quebec's ever-vigilant language cops who were out chasing English-language signs again. But how could I give it some fresh life? Then, one morning, I woke up and read about the latest motorcycle gang drug bust by the Quebec provincial police, a far less effective body than our language cops. Eureka! I had an angle. In my *Montreal Gazette* column, I opened like this:

> Every time I pick up the paper there's another story about Quebec's biker war: a three-year battle that's seen 48 murders, 240 bombs and enough drugs seized by police to pay off the federal deficit.
>
> Yet despite the endless police dragnets, the charges rarely stick and the motorcycle wars continue. It's becoming obvious the police are no match for the gangs—so who is? I have the solution. It's time we threw Quebec's most-committed government agency at the problem.
>
> Why not sic the language police on the bikers?

> Our province's tongue-troopers are an elite force of bureaucrats who've exhausted everyone from Jewish deli owners to Vietnamese *dépanneurs*. They've brought some of the largest corporations in the country to their knees—from Eaton (formerly Eaton's) to Poulet Frit Kentucky (formerly Colonel Sander's).
>
> But in recent years there are fewer English signs to chase and more inspectors around to chase them. Let's send them someplace they're really needed.

A fresh angle makes writing a lot easier and much more fun, but whether you have one or not, there are other elements that can help breathe some life into any story.

Every journalist knows the process starts with the "lead," the crucial few words, sentences or images that get a reader hooked.

The Art of the Opening: A good story is a bit like a seduction in which you slowly pull readers/viewers in with your wit and charm—and don't reveal your true personality until they've invested so much time they might be a little more tolerant of your flaws.

Every journalist knows the process starts with the "lead," the crucial few words, sentences or images that get a reader hooked. It's like those pickup lines boys learn when they're in high school and want a girl to dance—a few zingers to get them on the dance floor. Later you'll have to stand or fall on your own—on your personality, charm, substance and style. But you won't get a chance if you can't get them onto the floor, and the opening line is your most important move.

Traditionally most news stories opened with the five W's, but in recent years we've come to rely on another popular favourite—the individual human-interest lead intended to make any story seem relevant to the "local" reader. You've seen it so often, it's easy to parody: "Guelph, Ontario, native Mrs. Priscilla Pumpkin was one of 3 Canadians who died yesterday, along with over 17,000 Japanese when a volcano erupted on the island of Hokkaido, destroying much of it."

The human-interest lead works fine when the individual example is fascinating or relevant, but these days it's been so overused it's lost its individuality. If we keep it up much longer, we'll face a serious shortage of people who *haven't* been used in a lead.

Why not be a bit more creative? All you really need is an original thought or a catchy line that grabs the audience's attention. Tom Wolfe once wrote a story about a group of women in a detention centre and started the story as they stared out of their open cell window and tried to guess the name of the men who passed by down on the street. His opening sentence was: "Hai-ai-ai-ai-ai-ai-ai-ai-ai-ai-ai-aireeeeeeeeeee!"

That'll get your attention. So will this opening from "Passing the Time" by Alden Nowlan, published in the May 1975 issue of *Maclean's:*

> The first thing I learned about politics as a child in rural Nova Scotia was that you got paid for your vote. Before I knew the name of the prime minister I knew that on election day a local ward heeler would drive into the yard with a two-dollar bill for my grandmother and a bottle of rum for my father. Sometimes two ward heelers came, a Grit and a Tory, one after the other, and sat down in our kitchen smoking cigars. then my father, already half-drunk from his first pint, would manoeuvre with transparent slyness for a second.
>
> "No, no, Sam, I ain't been to vote yet; kinda thought mebbe I wouldn't bother with it this time."

In his book *Give War a Chance,* P. J. O'Rourke, always a strong starter, begins a story out of the Middle East at the time of the Gulf War with:

> War! War! Blood-red savage war! ... Saddam Hussein—he's worse than Hitler, worse than Stalin, worse than waking up wearing a wedding ring next to Roseanne Barr. He invaded Iran. He invaded Kuwait. He even invaded some parts of the country he already lives in, that's how crazy Saddam Hussein is. He's got chemical weapons filled with ... *chemicals*. Maybe he's got The Bomb. And missiles that can reach Riyadh, Tel Aviv. Spokane. Stock up on non-perishable foodstuffs.... We're all going to die. Details at eleven.

Still reading? Of course. So now what?

Writing to Be Read: Just because you've captured the readers' attention doesn't guarantee they'll stick around. Even after a sizzling lead, many stories get thick and hard to get through, filled with dense sentences penned by writers who dream of being William Faulkner but don't have the time (or talent) he did.

The simplest way to get your point across is with simple sentences. They're easy to read. They encourage you to get to the point. Most important, they force you to separate your ideas and figure out what you're trying to say. A long sentence can be a fine literary thing, but it requires you to know what you want to say and think through your sentence structure in advance, so your point doesn't get lost in your sentence's long, tantalizing striptease; the longer the sentence, the more likely you are to get to the end and forget what you were saying when you began, and by that time you're often too rushed by deadline to go back and figure it out and, well, you get my point.

In TV and documentary pieces, the right choice of words is almost as important as in print, but they can't steal the thunder from the images, which are the medium's real grammar.

The late Chicago columnist Mike Royko was always a master of plainspeak. His short, catchy style packs plenty of punch, as in this piece, "Daley Dissected," about then Chicago mayor and political boss Richard J. Daley. It's taken from *I Could Be Wrong, but I Doubt It:*

> Daley likes to build big things. He likes highrises, expressways, parking garages, municipal buildings and anything else that requires a ribbon-cutting ceremony and can be financed through federal funds. He isn't that enthusiastic about small things, such as people.
>
> Nepotism is big. Half the top officeholders are sons of former officeholders. Even the crime syndicate has its men in government. Everyone can join in if they do what they are told.
>
> It is truly democratic in a dictatorial sort of way.

Imagery helps, too. Metaphors and similes take work to find, but they're usually worth it because they let readers involve their own imagination in the story. If you're describing an accountant at work, does he study his tax records like someone who recently took a speed-reading course, or like a scholar examining the Dead Sea scrolls? Give it some time. Your first thought may be to describe a well-dressed gardener as "surprisingly dapper," but it's better to pause a moment and make him positively "rakish."

Tiny, telling details are part of what makes good journalistic writing. You need to use your senses to see, hear and sense small things that reveal personality and make up a scene: the photographs on someone's desk that show him posing with important people, the books on the wall, the framed letter from Mom.

Some reporters will say, "Look, I'm just not very observant," but anyone can see this stuff if they just look around. In life I'm often as unobservant as a lamppost, a guy with no sense of smell and bad hearing, who can't remember the colour of his son's eyes unless he's looking at them. But when I go out on a story I just turn on my internal camera and sound kit and stare at everything until I see something interesting: posters on walls, photos, clothing, shoes, socks, even underwear—if they're sticking out of someone's jeans. If I can see telling details, anyone can.

The rhythm of your writing can keep a reader going, too, the *rat-tat-tat* of the words and syllables rising and falling, building up excitement, then ever so slowly cooling things down. Even the tone of a story's writing can help pull the reader inside the world of the subject. TV reporter Tom Alderman has also written many lively magazine pieces, including a classic in the May 20, 1971, issue of the *Canadian* about former prime minister John Diefenbaker. In it Alderman uses the device of adopting Diefenbaker's own speech pattern and rhythm to give an inside view of the man:

> No indeed, thought Dief, there were still battles to be fought, people to be put in their place. The misguided were still cranking out books critical of his administration. History must be set right. What better spot to defend himself than his fourth-floor office in the centre block of the parliament buildings.... Here he could sit and anticipate the sallies of the misinformed. And prepare his memoirs, his exact, precise memoirs, replete with facts and names he had not yet revealed and evidence to date concealed, indisputable logic borne out and vindicated by time.

Alderman is one of many print reporters I know who easily made the leap to TV, but the reverse voyage is long and hard. Print forces you to write and structure your stories, while in TV it's possible to get by just linking images and interviews with a script that fills in the worst holes. Many of the best TV and radio reporters have done a stint in print—learning how to use words before they start worrying about pictures.

In TV and documentary pieces, the right choice of words is almost as important as in print, but they can't steal the thunder from the images, which are the medium's real grammar. In TV most of the superficial information is seen by the eye, and the script is more the subtext, telling you what isn't visible inside the frame.

Famed National Film Board documentary filmmaker Donald Brittain was really one of the best journalists Canada ever produced. He told stories on the screen, but the words in his scripts were much of the genius behind the pictures.

In his classic film *Paperland*, the opening is a long shot of a man skating toward us down Ottawa's Rideau Canal. As he approaches, we see that he wears a business suit and carries an attaché case. The script says:

> Here he comes now, trying to act like a normal human being. But he is that most despised of human creatures. His activities have brought down upon his shoulders the scorn and outrage of history's multitudes. He is homo bureaucratis, a bureaucrat, and he lives in a land of paper.
>
> He is the paper-pusher of the world, the administrator, the regulator, the co-ordinator ... He has been compared to the cockroach. Like the cockroach, he appears to have no useful function. Like the cockroach, he has many enemies. Like the cockroach, he has survived all attempt at extermination.
>
> This one's name is Bob Tewsley.

Yet sometimes, when TV images are really strong, the best words are no words. When the CBC's Brian Stewart showed the first shots of the terrible African famine a decade ago, an endless river of emaciated bodies walking in search for food, the images were shown silently over several minutes.

Stewart and his producers knew there really were no words that could match the power of the images. The pictures were so harrowing the words were best left for the viewer to provide.

Hey! Get your hands off that clicker. This essay isn't over yet.

Humour Helps: Among my own readers and viewers, I'm probably best-known for using humour, something I hesitate to talk about because it can kill the magic as surely as a magician explaining his tricks.

No matter what medium you work in, a smile is a wonderful way to help readers/viewers keep going. We've all started reading a piece on the meaning of the GATT agreement, then put it aside partway through with a yawn and a promise to go back to it afterward.

But a little humour can give readers a break that allows them to keep reading. I've always thought a smile is worth 100 words: it gives people renewed energy to keep watching another minute, or reading another two paragraphs.

The nice part of journalism is you don't even have to be amusing; you can let your subject be amusing for you. Much has been written about the art of the tough question, but some of the nicest moments in interviews are the small spontaneous times when a person lights up with a smile or shares an infectious laugh that makes you join in.

Or when someone says something funny in the middle of an otherwise serious interview. We all need these moments in life, and they're just as important in a métier that purports to "cover" life. I know some journalists worry that if they add a light touch they won't be taken seriously, but life is often serious and funny at the same time.

A smile can also be a subversive weapon, because it lowers your audience's resistance and let's you sneak under its guard. Often you can make people laugh at something they may not even agree with, if you give them a chance to think about it. Humour is a great way to get by the ideological gatekeeper at everyone's mental door, to get them suddenly laughing at something they didn't know they'd find funny.

Humour can enlist even reluctant readers/viewers as momentary allies, pulling them onside and making them realize their own ideas aren't always as entrenched as they thought. In Quebec, my neck of the woods, humour is a useful device because it unites English and French, federalists and sovereignists, allowing them to laugh at the same things even when they disagree on them. If you indignantly attack Quebec's language law for allowing signs that are only half as large in English as in French, Anglos may cheer but French readers will quickly turn the page. Yet start your column off in French, followed by an English translation in half-size print, and both sides will probably chuckle and read on.

Where does one go to "find" humour? I tend to look for what's not obvious, what runs contrary to grain: the fisherman who hates fish; the compulsively talkative mime. When I was in the Arctic a number of years ago, filming a documentary about various expeditions trying to get to the North Pole, I didn't pay much attention to all the grit, sweat and determination of the guys grunting and sweating on their dogsleds.

I'd seen that on TV a thousand times. What stuck in my mind was that the expert on helping them all mount their expeditions was the late Basel Jesudasen, an East Asian from the steamy Indian city of Madras, who lived in the High Arctic and knew more about getting to the North Pole than the Inuit themselves. Basel's presence had changed the Arctic in small ways as the Arctic had changed him. For instance, many Inuit in his town ate their Arctic char with chutney, a custom they'd picked up dining at Basel's place.

It's details like that that stand out and break stereotypes, that make you rethink the clichés. They make the North seem less and more heroic. More human. More complicated.

Journalist George Plimpton's book *Paper Lion,* about his brief stint training for the NFL's Detroit Lions, works well partly because as a gangly academic-type guy with an upper-class accent, Plimpton is such an unlikely-looking quarterback. Throughout his book, you're waiting for Plimpton to get flattened, as you know he should, and it's that hope for his flattening that leads you on. It adds a humorous subtext to even the most serious moments of his football sociology.

> The ball slapped into my palm at "three." I turned and started back. I could feel my balance going, and two yards behind the line of scrimmage *I fell down*—absolutely flat, as if my feet had been pinned under a trip wire stretched across the field, not a hand laid on me. I heard a great roar go up from the crowd. Suffused as I had been with confidence, I could scarcely believe what had happened . . . the mortification beginning to come fast. I rose

hurriedly to my knees at the referee's whistle and I could see my teammates' big silver helmets with the blue Lion decals turn toward me . . .

I joined the huddle. "Sorry, sorry," I said.

"Call the play, man," came a voice from one of the helmets.

"I don't know what happened," I said.

"Call it, man."

Even as you hear Plimpton crying, you can't help but chuckle.

The Finish Line. One of the most disappointing things in a good story is to get all the way to the end and suddenly be cut off in mid-stride by an abrupt or lazy ending—to be left stranded in emotional midair. In fiction it's an accepted rule that you close dramatically, then give a little time for the readers/viewers to let it all sink in. The same should be true for journalism. A skillful closing adds a finishing touch to any good story. It should cast light on everything you've read, make you think, or sigh, or just smile.

Yet while most journalists are obsessed with the lead, they sometimes give little thought to the closing. There are many reasons for this: journalists who are used to editors who cut from the end of a story; journalists who have just run out of time. Or energy. Or ideas.

I've always thought that when the readers/viewers get to the end of a piece they should be disappointed they can't turn the page and read a little more. At the end of one of P. J. O'Rourke's anti-Russian rants collected in *Give War a Chance,* he closes like this:

> Lots of countries are poor and lots are dreary and oppressive. But the Soviet Union is a huge, healthy nation with more than 20 million college graduates. It has all the land and mineral resources that national avarice could imagine. And Russia has been part of—at least an idiot stepsister to—Western civilization for a thousand years. There's no alibi for the place.

Likewise, there's no alibi for a poor ending except the failure to give it the extra minute of thought you probably gave the lead. And what a shame if your readers or viewers stick with you all the way to the end just to be disappointed.

A good ending is to a journalist what a good dessert is to a chef. It's the last thing your customers will remember. If you've put a lot of effort into your appetizers and the entrée, why not leave your patrons dreaming about the next meal instead of disappointed by an unfinished flan?

The above suggestions are ones that have worked for me and some other journalists and cannot be guaranteed. There is, I repeat, no formula for How to Become a Great Writer. But if you do come across one, please send it to me via the publisher and I'll send you three payments of $29.95 (plus shipping and handling costs). I'm always looking for new tricks.

Okay, you can change essays now.

SALLY AW SIAN

Sally Aw Sian, O.B.E., J.P., Hon. LL.D., is the chairwoman and chief executive officer of the Sing Tao Group, which engages mainly in publishing and printing. Under Dr. Aw's leadership since 1951, the *Sing Tao Daily*, the group's principal newspaper, has grown and developed into the first international Chinese-language paper.

For two terms, Dr. Aw was chairwoman of the International Press Institute. By encouraging fellowship among world journalists, she has made lasting contributions to international journalism. In recognition of Dr. Aw's distinguished achievements in world publishing, the E. W. Scripps School of Journalism at Ohio University conferred its prestigious Carr Van Anda Award on her in 1988.

The founding of the Sing Tao School of Journalism at the University of British Columbia and the donation of a new building to the E. W. Scripps School of Journalism at Ohio University are two examples of Dr. Aw's generous support to education in journalism.

An Interview with Sally Aw Sian

QUESTION: Could you describe the extent of the newspaper holdings that you inherited from your father, Aw Boon Haw?

DR. AW: From my father I inherited the Sing Tao morning and evening dailies and the *Hong Kong Standard.*

QUESTION: Could you describe how the Sing Tao Group has grown since you took it over at the age of 21?

DR. AW: The first paper to be added was the *Sing Tao Daily* in New York in 1965. In 1972 the company went public, and in 1975, Sing Tao dailies were added in San Francisco, London and other cities in Europe. The first Canadian edition was in Toronto in 1978, then came Sydney, Australia, in 1982; Vancouver in 1983; and Auckland, New Zealand in 1991.

QUESTION: You have said that the expansion to North America came, in part, by chance. Could you tell us about that?

DR. AW: I first got the idea for overseas editions from talking to people when I travelled. Chinese immigrants were forever asking me what was new in Hong Kong. I then set about to create Sing Tao dailies in the cities where the numbers of Chinese immigrants were increasing. In the case of Canada, it was mostly after the 1967 riot in Hong Kong.

QUESTION: Could you explain the concept behind the Sing Tao Group of newspapers? Who is your audience and is the guiding philosophy now any different than it was when the *Sing Tao Daily* first went international?

DR. AW: The concept behind the *Sing Tao Daily,* when started by my father, was to present the Chinese viewpoint, since there was no media that did that. Now the readership is more sophisticated and we have changed our emphasis to real-estate, computer and financial news.

QUESTION: Did your father instill in you a love of the business, or did you ever think of doing something else with your life?

DR. AW: I was put in the position and I was interested in the business. I never thought of doing anything else.

QUESTION: Aside from the obvious financial success, what other satisfactions has the newspaper business brought you?

DR. AW: I enjoy the service that we have been able to provide to the community. For instance, we sponsor a scholarship student loan fund, we campaign for the poor during Chinese New Year, and there are other community projects that help people.

QUESTION: With respect to the endowments you have given to universities and the like, you have said that it is Sing Tao's corporate philosophy "to give back to the communities that have helped you grow." Could you explain?

DR. AW: My family has always believed it was important to be involved with the community. We like to help in any way we can.

QUESTION: What led you to become interested in journalism education and to invest in its future?

DR. AW: I have been interested in journalism education all along and feel that continual education training will elevate the standard of journalism and help to create better newspapers.

QUESTION: What kind of education do you think today's journalists need?

DR. AW: Today's journalists need to be more creative and to be more responsible, as well. There aren't any big-name journalists anymore in print. Possibly it is because most of them switch to the electronic media. There needs to be more emphasis on the print media.

QUESTION: What is your opinion of the standards and ethics of modern-day journalism?

DR. AW: I feel they are on the decline. The trend is to report the news without sufficient background and without really getting to the root of the story. There has definitely been a decline in standards and ethics during the time I have been in business. Journalists need to be concerned about this and put more effort into what they do. They should also be more accountable.

QUESTION: Are you concerned about the trend toward concentration of ownership?

DR. AW: I am concerned, but concentrated ownership enables more papers to survive. However, readers should be concerned because it may mean that there are not enough independent viewpoints.

QUESTION: What do you think about the future of newspapers in light of the development of new media, principally the Internet?

DR. AW: The future of newspapers is still there. The Internet will not be able to replace newspapers yet because we still have to sit in front of the computer to watch it. It is not mobile enough to carry with you wherever you go.

QUESTION: Earlier this year you sold 50 percent of your Canadian operation to Torstar Corporation. Aside from the financial benefit, are there journalistic benefits for both companies?

DR. AW: Yes, first of all, we will become a genuinely Canadian company. We will also be able to get much more Canadian news, and there are mutual benefits in such areas as promotion and subscriptions.

QUESTION: At the present time Asia is experiencing economic difficulties. What are your predictions for the economic future of Asia?

DR. AW: Asia's future is good. The present difficulties will last for a year or two, then a recovery will take place. Asians are generally known to be very resourceful and resilient. They always find ways and means to turn around and make a full recovery.

QUESTION: You told an interviewer in 1988 that you intended to retire in five years. That was 10 years ago. As someone who is a self-confessed workaholic and who is utterly fascinated by the business world, what will you do with your time when, and if, you retire?

DR. AW: There will be a lot of interesting work for me to do, especially on the philanthropy side. Through the foundation that is named after my parents, I will be helping in the fields of education, medicine and care for the aged.